Maternity H

For Unmarried Mothers

A community service

Maud Morbclock,

Hilary Campbell

Alpha Editions

This edition published in 2020

ISBN : 9789354027871

Design and Setting By
Alpha Editions
email - alphaedis@gmail.com

As per information held with us this book is in Public Domain.
This book is a reproduction of an important historical work. Alpha Editions
uses the best technology to reproduce historical work in the same manner
it was first published to preserve its original nature. Any marks or number
seen are left intentionally to preserve its true form.

Contents

Illustrations by Constance Dillon

MATERNITY HOMES
FOR UNMARRIED MOTHERS

a community service

by **MAUD MORLOCK** and **HILARY CAMPBELL**

1946

THE FIRST STEP in helping a baby born out of wedlock to get a start in life without the legal and social handicaps that society still imposes for illegitimate birth is to make available to his mother during pregnancy, at delivery, and while she is planning her future and the future of her baby whatever advice and assistance she needs. That is one of the Children's Bureau's interests in maternity homes for unmarried mothers. Another of its interests is that unmarried mothers receive the same high quality of maternity care—prenatal, delivery, and postpartum—that all mothers should have and that the baby have good medical and nursing care. It is possible for these two interests, the life-long social welfare of mother and child and a high standard of maternal and infant care for them, to find fulfillment in maternity-home care. Both factors are discussed in this bulletin.

In *Maternity Homes for Unmarried Mothers* the homes are discussed as a community service. The bulletin is intended primarily, of course, for the inner circle of boards of directors and the advisory committees they appoint, for example, medical advisory committees, and for the staffs of homes and of the case-work agencies that work with them. It will be of value also, we hope, to State and local departments of health or welfare, which by law in many States have responsibility for licensing and supervising maternity homes, and to councils of social agencies in helping the homes strengthen their programs.

Certain parts of the bulletin may be of use to social agencies other than case-work agencies, for example, to youth-serving organizations; to public-health agencies such as visiting-nurse associations; and to some individuals who, because of their professions or occupations, are likely to give the first advice to illegitimately pregnant young women, that is, individuals who are physicians, nurses, lawyers, clergymen, teachers, personnel directors, or employers.

The Children's Bureau wishes to acknowledge with thanks the help of all those who read the manuscript. They made many invaluable suggestions.

Maud Morlock, Social Service Division, and Hilary Campbell, Division of Reports, wrote the bulletin except for the section, *Health and Medical Services*. Miss Morlock is consultant in services to unmarried mothers. *Health and Medical Services* was prepared by Barbara A. Hewell, M.D., Division of Research in Child Development, in cooperation with John L. Parks, M.D., the Bureau's consultant in obstetrics, and Marjorie M. Heseltine, consultant in nutrition, Division of Health Services.

Katharine F. Lenroot

Chief, Children's Bureau

History—Prologue to the Present

Two hundred years of the social history of the United States—as a colony and as a republic—had woven their changing pattern into the Nation's life before protection was offered to unmarried mothers in shelters definitely for them. During the two centuries in which this new tolerance was slowly germinating, harsh punishment for the mother and denial of legal rights to her child were the general rule. The stigma placed on mother and child is an old, old story—much older than two centuries. The stigma is as old as the institution of marriage, which it is imposed to protect. Society hoped to prevent illegitimate births by the severity of its punishment and of its legal discriminations. It took no cognizance of causes or of the innocence of the child. This solid wall of illogic had to be razed. Individuals and groups who saw the role of society and the law as protective rather than punitive have made a breach.

ATTITUDES TOWARD MOTHER AND CHILD

This bulletin deals with one part of the effort to break through this wall of illogic surrounding illegitimate birth—maternity-home service to an unmarried mother through her travail and her planning for the future. First will be shown, briefly, public attitudes and their expressions in social care of mother or child—or the lack of it—during the two hundred years before maternity homes came into being. Later the bulletin presents for consideration the program of service of the home of today, including case work, group activities, and health and medical services, and outlines the organization of a home.

In colonial days

Attitudes in pre-Revolutionary New England toward illegitimate birth stemmed from two sources. The religious code of the Puritan settlers was predominant, but closely allied to this stern judgment was the necessity for protecting from dependency the decidedly slender resources of a community pioneering in a land of short summers and stubborn soil. Legal punishment naturally followed the law of the mother country, England. Naturally, too, the colonists tried to apply the English laws on dependency to their own conditions but with a determination to prevent what they thought of as the permanent pauperism of the old country. They wanted everyone in the new settlements to take a fair share in the conquest of the wilderness.

In English law, followed in the colonies, the mother of a child born out of wedlock was known as a "lewd" woman and her child as a "bastard." In Puritan settlements the mother might be required to confess her sin before the congregation. She might be publicly whipped, placed in stocks, or imprisoned. Even after she had suffered her legal punishment, her social punishment continued in ostracism. To help her or the child would, it was believed, increase the number of illegitimate births. The punishment prescribed for Hester Prynne in Nathaniel Hawthorne's *The Scarlet Letter*—the lifelong wearing of the letter "A" for "adulteress"—is fact, not fancy. This penalty will be found among the laws of Plymouth Colony for 1658.

The cruel treatment of unmarried mothers and their children often resulted in the concealment by the mother of her pregnancy and the consequent lack of physical care, abortion, the death of the mother in childbirth, the suicide of the young woman, the abandonment of the baby, or even the crime of infanticide. Concealment by the mother of death of a child born out of wedlock was punishable by death unless the mother could prove by the testimony of a witness that the child was born dead. Effie Deans in Sir Walter Scott's *The Heart of Midlothian*, based on actual happenings in the Edinburgh of 1736, was sentenced to death for the supposed death of her baby boy at birth. He had actually been stolen and was found as a youth. Under Scottish law the young woman could have been saved at her trial from the death penalty by testimony that she had told her family of her pregnancy before the baby's birth. The devoutly truthful sister, Jeanie, who could not bring herself to swear falsely that Effie had told her,

2

later walked from Edinburgh to London to win a pardon for the younger girl.

Although an element in the legal harshness toward the child was the desire to protect public funds, the father of the child actually faced little inconvenience. His responsibility was difficult to prove and his support seldom ordered. The burden of support was placed on the mother. If she could not carry it, the child was exposed to whatever methods the community had in caring for dependent children. The baby of illegitimate birth whose mother could not support him was frequently neglected by the community and always, as he grew, treated as a social outcast.

Foundlings and children of all ages who became dependent on public support were usually placed out in families by the process of indenture, borrowed from England. Under this contract they were to be cared for and taught an occupation and later were to repay the expense of their care and training by work.

Children in almshouses

Almshouses, the first public institutions in the American colonies, came into existence as early as 1660. They sheltered dependent and neglected children, many of whom were of illegitimate birth, as well as poverty-stricken adults. This was true for over 200 years when Massachusetts started placing children in family homes. With no differentiation, the handicapped, the insane, the feeble-minded, the aged, the vicious, the sick, and the homeless were all herded together in crowded quarters. The overcrowding caused rapid spread of disease, especially among children. The only care the children received, sick or well, was from the older inmates. Child mortality was very high. Those who survived knew only life in a pauper institution. If they were taught at all it was by ignorant employees.

Most of the foundlings placed in almshouses for shelter were of illegitimate birth. The death rate of these babies was exceedingly high during the whole history of these unclassified institutions. In the early days of a Massachusetts State almshouse, founded in 1854, between 80 and 90 percent of the foundlings sent there died within a year in spite of the best care known at that time.

Private foster care for children

The nineteenth century opened with the public authorities apprenticing dependent children, many of whom were born out of wedlock, to families by indenture, or keeping them in almshouses with adults. Meanwhile, however, private religious agencies not under church auspices had been developing foster care of children concurrently with

3

the growth of almshouses. Their wards were dependent for the same reasons as children in almshouses. Many of these institutions for orphans were intended as temporary shelters until the children could be placed in families to learn trades. They were better than almshouses only because they separated children from the insane, the vicious, the sick and other adult inmates of almshouses. At least 26 institutions for destitute children are known to have been established before 1825, and at least 80 more before 1850. Some of the early homes were special institutions for children who were physically or mentally handicapped. This segregation of children from the mixed almshouse was plainly one step forward toward a recognition of the fact that dependent children need care different from the care given to adult dependents.

The beginning of the child-placing agency is of great significance to the later establishment of maternity homes for unmarried mothers, which are concerned with the future of the child as well as of the mother. This start came about during the second half of the nineteenth century along with a great acceleration of the founding of institutions under religious and secular auspices. Children's aid societies came into being as early as 1853, and had their greatest growth during the 1880's in eastern cities. The children's homefinding movement spread through the midwest and northwest. One of the services offered was the sending of homeless children to farm families in the middle western States. This method of placement in free homes or for adoption recognized the fact that the usual experiences of life in an ordinary family are better preparation for earning a living than institutional training. In practice, the chief drawbacks of these placements were that the agencies failed to safeguard the welfare of the children; took children from their own homes, if parents requested it; kept inadequate records; knew nothing of the homes the children went into; and failed to follow up placements. These beginnings have grown into the network of child-placing agencies of today whose services will be mentioned frequently in the section, *The Value of Case-Work Service.*

Substitutes for public almshouses

The middle of the nineteenth century also witnessed the development of State and local institutions as substitutes for almshouse care of children. By this time, the full horror of these mixed almshouses as places for children was recognized by some groups of public-spirited citizens, but shelter had to be planned for the children released from almshouses. A number of States began to give subsidies to private agencies to provide care for dependent children. A few States established by law a State-wide system of county homes. Local institutions were created in counties or in cities in a number of other States, but

4

local care was more often provided by private institutions receiving public funds.

During this period, Massachusetts made public-welfare history in two ways. In 1863, it created the Board of State Charities to supervise its whole system of public charities. This was the first State department of public welfare. In its second report, the new board recommended a reclassification of State almshouses and the separation of children from contacts with adults. The second step came 4 years after the board's establishment when Massachusetts began to place its young dependent wards in boarding homes. Other States followed the example of Massachusetts during the latter part of the nineteenth century.

State responsibility

This trend toward recognition of the responsibility of the State for the well-being of individuals has developed consistently. State governments in recent years have shown active concern for a greater variety of social problems. Structure and organization are being developed in State governments that make possible social services and facilities for all people in need of them.

Today, every State in the Union has a State department of public welfare with a bureau or division charged with the welfare of children, including those born out of wedlock. This division of the State department of welfare helps counties or other local units to build up child-welfare services, which include, of course, services to unmarried mothers and their babies.

Federal assistance

The outstanding development of recent years in public services to children is the assistance of the Federal Government in the extension and strengthening of the service, made possible by the passage of the Social Security Act in 1935. Provisions of the act make funds available to States for establishing, extending, and strengthening public child-welfare services, especially in rural areas or in areas of special need. Local, State, and Federal funds make possible the employment of qualified child-welfare workers in communities that had never organized services for their children. As yet, many communities are without these services because the funds available are insufficient for a program reaching throughout the Nation. If services were provided in every county, specialized help would be available to an unmarried mother from the moment she asked advice from this source of counsel through the various stages of her care and that of her baby.

The maternity homes should see their services in relation to the total child-welfare program. Application for maternity-home care, sometimes in homes located at a distance from the community where a mother lives, can be made by or received by the child-welfare worker who then can provide service before and after the period of care in the maternity home. Also, children of unmarried mothers may receive assistance under the provisions of the Social Security Act for aid to dependent children,

MATERNITY HOMES GET UNDER WAY

The first institutions that could be considered maternity homes for unmarried mothers were founded in the middle of the nineteenth century to shelter and to "reform" unmarried mothers and to give physical care to their babies. These institutions were usually under religious auspices or motivation.

Obscurity of early history

It is exceedingly difficult to trace the history of those early homes or even to determine the dates of their origin. Some of them have gone out of existence leaving no history behind; others that once served unmarried mothers now provide other types of care and have no definite record of their earlier work; and still others that now do this work, originally served a different purpose.

Today, the number of maternity homes for unmarried mothers in the United States is estimated at 200. During a search for the historical beginnings of this movement, a list of maternity homes now in existence, and for which the date of founding was obtainable, was checked against various sources. Although the information so obtained gives an incomplete picture, it does show that of 123 homes listed, 13 were founded before 1870; 7 between 1870 and 1880; 12 between 1880 and 1890; 51 between 1890 and 1900; and 40 since 1900. That is, about two-thirds started their work during the nineteenth century—the majority of these during the last decade of that century—and one-third during the twentieth century.

Under Catholic auspices

Homes for the specific care of unmarried mothers did not develop until the middle of the nineteenth century. A very early protective service for young women afforded by the Roman Catholic Church seems to have forecast the concern that later grew into Catholic homes for unmarried mothers. Late in 1842 a band of Sisters of the Good

6

Shepherd arrived in the United States from their motherhouse in France, their destination being Louisville, Kentucky. In this work, no matter how depraved a woman might have been, they did not give up hope for her.[1] The part of the Sisters' work that touches the history of maternity homes was of a preventive nature—protection in the convent of young women "who had committed no offenses but who were exposed to temptations of wrong doing." The Sisters' program was based on three elements, religion, work, and education. In a short time their services became widely known and various bishops appealed to the Louisville house for the establishment of similar work in their dioceses. In response, the Sisters of the Good Shepherd established convents in Philadelphia and St. Louis within seven years of their arrival in this country.

The immediate predecessors of Catholic homes for unmarried mothers were shelters opened for abandoned or orphaned babies during a serious cholera epidemic at the height of immigration from Ireland and Germany about the middle of the century. Roman Catholic leaders realized that the existing Catholic institutions for children were not suitable for the care of babies: general hospitals provided the only shelter for foundlings under Catholic auspices. One of these hospitals, St. Mary's in Buffalo, N. Y., started a small separate shelter for babies. From this specialized care of foundlings grew the logical realization that the care of their mothers was inseparably bound up with the fate of the babies. Fewer babies would be abandoned if their mothers had a place of refuge. Shortly after St. Mary's started its separate homes for babies, about 1852, the Sisters began to provide shelter and care for unmarried mothers. The next institution for the care of foundlings to be established, St. Ann's in St. Louis, began with this idea, namely, that one of the best means of saving a baby was by offering shelter to the mother.

Two Roman Catholic infant and maternity homes were opened before 1855; 7 between 1855 and 1870; 6 between 1870 and 1890; 15 between 1890 and 1910; and 14 between 1910 and 1930.

Under Protestant auspices

Homes were undoubtedly being opened under Protestant or nonsectarian auspices at about the same time that the Catholic homes were being founded, but their history was seldom recorded. One of the earliest of these, still in existence, is the Talitha Cumi Maternity Home and Hospital in Boston, organized in 1836.

About one group of homes, however, the Florence Crittenton, a good deal has been written and their development can be readily fol-

---

[1] Catholic Charities in the United States; history and problems, by John O'Grady. National Conference of Catholic Charities, Washington, D. C. 1930. 475 pp.

lowed. As the history of this group undoubtedly parallels in many respects that of other homes founded during the last two decades of the nineteenth century, a glance at its history will give an idea of the history of them all.[2]

Florence Crittenton homes

Charles N. Crittenton, a successful business man, began this "rescue work" for women in memory of his daughter Florence, who died in childhood. He opened the first Florence Night Mission in the heart of the New York vice district in 1883. Here he held religious services for "outcast girls," as part of his effort to redeem, through religious conversion, prostitutes and other "fallen" women. Being practical, he soon realized, however, that a woman receiving the classical advice "go and sin no more" might have no place to go.

Charles Crittenton's next move was a step toward prevention. He established in New York a home in which working girls away from their families might be safe from the dangers common to some of the poorer boarding houses. This idea grew into the founding of rescue homes for unmarried mothers.

Ten years after he started his work, Charles Crittenton met Kate Waller Barrett. As the wife of a clergyman, Mrs. Barrett had seen the harsh treatment inflicted upon many unmarried mothers and had become active in their "rescue." She had already opened a home for unmarried mothers in Atlanta, overcoming great resistence from some groups in that city who thought unmarried mothers should not be helped. Working together, Mr. Crittenton and Mrs. Barrett planned and started a Nation-wide Florence Crittenton organization which was granted a national charter in 1898 by a special act of Congress.

Thirteen Florence Crittenton homes had been established by 1893, 10 of which were in operation in 1933 when the history of the movement was written. In 1945, 48 maternity homes were affiliated with The National Florence Crittenton Mission.

The constitution of the new organization specified that homes granted the use of the Florence Crittenton name should conform to five principles: (1) The government of the home shall be Christian and parental in character; (2) the property purchased shall be used for all time for the purpose for which it was acquired; (3) no debts shall be incurred, except for current expenses, without the consent of the national organization; (4) everything possible shall be done to keep mother and child together; (5) the mother shall be required to stay in the home at least 6 months after the birth of the child.

In 1895, Charles Crittenton bought a private railroad car in which

[2] Fifty Years' Work with Girls 1883–1933, by Otto Wilson in collaboration with Robert South Barrett. The National Florence Crittenton Mission, Alexandria, Va. 1933.

he traveled over the country holding evangelistic services and urging the establishment of rescue homes. As in the case of all pioneers, it took courage on the part of Mr. Crittenton and Mrs. Barrett to attack this social problem, taboo in the conventional circles of that day.

Kate Waller Barrett, a woman ahead of the thought of her time, made an unusual contribution to services to unmarried mothers. Her understanding of their difficulties was, of course, warmly sympathetic, but also intellectual and thoroughly practical. She won her degree of doctor of medicine in order to be of greater use to the cause in which she worked so wholeheartedly. These two founders of the Florence Crittenton homes undoubtedly helped to turn the trend of public opinion away from placing a lifetime stigma on unmarried mothers and their babies.

Salvation Army homes and hospitals

The Salvation Army has long been concerned about the plight of unmarried mothers and is one of the most active organizations in their service. The Army is now operating 35 homes and hospitals for unmarried mothers in the United States.

The mission work founded in Great Britain in 1865 by the Rev. William Booth and his wife, Catherine, was first called the Salvation Army in 1878. Only 2 years later, the Army sent its first contingent of officers to Philadelphia to start the work of the organization in the United States. The pattern of work and of development has been much the same in the old and new countries. The Army's work, based on religion and aimed at the redemption of the "lost," spread from city to city as groups of citizens came to realize the unwholesome conditions in their city's "slums" and asked the Army to try to clear them up.

The maternity home for unmarried mothers is a natural outgrowth of the Salvation Army's early mission work for women. Women members of the Army originated the work under the leadership of Mrs. Bramwell Booth, the young daughter-in-law of the Army's founder and wife of the Chief of Staff. They went into the vice-ridden districts of London seeking "fallen" women—drunkards, narcotic addicts, and prostitutes—in the streets or brothels, begging them to begin a new life and helping all who were willing to try. Soon women were coming to the Army asking for shelter.

The early homes of the Salvation Army, the first opened in London in 1884, were places of refuge for these homeless, destitute, "debauched" women. Some who came, however, were bewildered, young expectant mothers, unmarried and cast out by all who knew them. They were different in experience from the other women in the homes, needing protection and medical care. Within a year the Army realized that a different place from the rescue homes was necessary for these unmarried mothers. Only the workhouse was open to them for the delivery of their babies and there they were thrown into exceedingly undesirable company. This realization brought about the opening of a small maternity home with space for six young women.

Three years after the work of the rescue homes began in England, Mrs. Bramwell Booth sent one of her officers to the United States to assist in the opening of the first rescue home here—in Brooklyn, N. Y. That same year, 1887, homes were opened also in Grand Rapids, Mich., and in Oakland, Calif. The young movement grew quickly. In 7 years 15 homes had been opened in the United States.

The pattern of services and of development of what is now the Women's Social Service Department was much the same as in Britain —first the "rescue" of the prostitute and other outcast women and later the segregation from them of young unmarried mothers who needed different care. The Salvation Army officers did hard, physical drudgery as well as work for spiritual redemption. They had only slender financial resources, begging food from commission houses in the markets and other necessities from individuals of means. They were inexperienced in the ways of the world and untrained for their work. But they had faith in the improvability of individuals and love and understanding to offer to the women society had cast out. Their faith gave them courage to challenge the deep-rooted social intolerance of their time and to lay the foundations for the service of today, the extent of which in physical care at least they could not have imagined.

Although the Salvation Army is a religious organization, it does not require those it serves to accept its religious point of view. Religion is a therapy offered to those in trouble, to be accepted or rejected at their will. Much of this therapy of religion reaches the residents of the Army's maternity homes through the way of life of the staff, as the Army believes that a sermon is more effective lived than preached.

CHANGING PHILOSOPHY OF MATERNITY-HOME CARE

The foregoing summary has shown first the harsh intolerance of former times toward unmarried mothers and children born out of wedlock and second the development of assistance for them, as groups of people began to realize the injustice of the cruelties they suffered and went to their help. Against this gradually shifting background the changes that have taken place in the philosophy of maternity-home care and the programs that grew out of these changes become clear. Philosophy and program, like public attitudes toward the woman illegitimately pregnant, have changed as life for young people, especially young women, has reached new stages of independence.

These changes in social customs have come fast since the 1880's when the maternity-home movement got under way. Industrialization of our economy took young people from the farms to cities. Youth now establishes independence from the parental home at an earlier age. Boys and girls go farther away from the home than they did. More education is available to more young people, and a wider range of employment is now open to them, particularly to women. The automobile has introduced new factors in behavior. Sex is more freely discussed by all ages. More and more parents and schools are giving young people sound sex education at the appropriate ages.

Repression as a cure

When maternity homes were starting their work, a woman who became pregnant out of wedlock was considered a "fallen" woman and a proper subject for reform. Maternity homes were places of refuge. This idea is still suggested by the names of some of the homes today —Door of Hope, House of Mercy, Sheltering Arms. Although the groups that founded maternity homes championed the cause of unmarried mothers and worked for more humane treatment of them, at the same time some homes limited the freedom of their residents— even opened their mail, a procedure that plainly showed a lack of confidence in them.

In the early years of maternity homes and other social agencies, illegitimate pregnancy was viewed solely as a moral problem, without the thought of economic, social, or emotional factors. The whole life experience of the individual was overshadowed by this one episode. Repression was the formula for cure; the approach to the young woman was moralistic. She was expected to keep her baby.

Deep-rooted causes

Today it is recognized that in practically every instance of illegitimate birth the situation is much more complex than appears on the surface. The first break with the earlier, stereotyped emphasis on sex behavior was an attempt to explain the problem in terms of environmental causes, that is, broken homes, low mentality, ignorance of parents, bad housing conditions, or lack of sex information on the part of young women. Although all of these adverse conditions may be factors, increasing knowledge of why people act as they do shows that illegitimate pregnancy involves not only the immediate situation but the whole life pattern of the individual, which starts at birth. This knowledge shows that young women who have had love and security in their own homes in childhood and adolescence through companionable relations with their parents, who have had wholesome interests, suitable education and recreation, and spiritual guidance are less likely to have a child without marriage.

Most maternity homes have recognized this growing knowledge of behavior as it affects the young women they serve. Deeper understanding of the difficulties that bring girls to them has led maternity home boards of directors and staffs to make their programs and procedures more flexible and more responsive to the differences in the situations presented. They have developed programs that stimulate new interests and develop individual skills in order to substitute for confused, youthful groping, the tools to build a more satisfying way of life.

Some homes, however, have been slow to use pertinent new techniques. These homes would want the latest medical knowledge used if one of their residents was ill with typhoid fever, in order to insure the recovery of the patient and to protect the other residents. They would go a step farther and cooperate with public-health authorities to discover the source of infection, however remote from the home it might be, for the safety of the community or even of other communities. They would accept the research work in all the sciences that have contributed to the present knowledge of typhoid fever, its transmission, and the methods for its prevention. Unfortunately, however, it seems to be hard for these same homes to accept new knowledge of why individuals act as they do and new ways of helping young people to find themselves.

Incompleteness of service

Few communities, in planning for maternity-home service, have taken into account the needs of women in racial minority groups. Only a few homes for their protection exist, in spite of the fact that these services should be for all unmarried mothers who need them. Furthermore, few communities afford mothers in minority groups adequate case-work service and foster-home care for their babies. Frequently, good medical care is not available to them. They may need financial aid even more than young women of the majority population whose relatives may be in better economic circumstances.

This lack of service stands out conspicuously, for example, when the welfare of Negro unmarried mothers and their babies is considered. Historically, little service for them was provided in the years reviewed here. An institution for dependent children of free Negro families was organized as early as 1822. Both the Society of Friends and the Roman Catholic Church were influential in the founding of some other institutions for Negro children. But relatively few had service of any kind until foster-home care for children came into use.

A few homes for Negro unmarried mothers have been established as a result of the interest of Negro women themselves in the conditions surrounding young women brought about by the mass migration of Negroes from rural areas to big cities. Later a few established maternity homes made arrangements for Negro unmarried mothers either in the home itself or in foster family homes.

AND NOW THE PRESENT

Giving assistance to unmarried mothers and their babies is only one aspect of the broader community program of services to families and children. That it is an important part is shown by the fact that approximately 80,000 live births out of wedlock are reported each year for the United States. The real figure is much larger because, it is commonly known, many illegitimate births are registered as legitimate, and 10 States, some of them with large populations, do not record legitimacy on birth certificates.

Figures are valuable as a basis for planning, but more significant than the figures are the human beings they represent. The question can be asked, "Who are these mothers, and what social conditions have contributed to the birth of these infants?" We know that more than half of the mothers come from rural areas which have little in the way of wholesome recreation or of social-service facilities. We know that illegitimacy is not confined to any one community group. For the most part the mothers are young, about one-half of the illegitimate births occurring to mothers of less than 19 years. Many of them are immature and still struggling with the problems of adolescence. Many have not had the affection and security in their own homes that are essential in the development of a child's personality. Some may have been employed, but in all probability they have not had much vocational training. Their earnings from unskilled work are barely sufficient for their own needs and there is often little margin for the support of a child.

The problem of the unmarried mother is complicated by the attitude of the girl and of her family toward bringing a child into the world against the code established by society. Both the parents and the girl may have feelings of guilt. They may also fear the attitude of friends and neighbors—and this fear may be sufficiently powerful to cause them to make unwise plans, particularly in regard to the placement of the baby,

If the child born out of wedlock is to have opportunity for normal growth and development, his needs as well as those of his mother and father must be met. He must be given a home where he will have security. This may be either with his own mother or a foster home that approximates as nearly as possible the home children normally have with their own parents.

We do not have statistical information as to how many of these infants are known to social agencies or how many of their mothers are being assisted in making plans for themselves and their babies.

In urban communities, social services of various kinds are usually available to the unmarried mother and her child. Under the provisions of the Social Security Act, many child-welfare workers are now employed in rural counties, or in areas of special need. Increasingly, more mothers are receiving early in pregnancy the help that they need. It is imperative that such service be extended to every area in the United States. Only then can we be assured that every unmarried mother and her baby will receive individualized assistance.

A local child-welfare worker can help the community to understand the needs of young people and to provide the resources that make for wholesome living. For those who get into difficulty, she can help to provide the necessary assistance. One resource among many that she will frequently use for the girl illegitimately pregnant is the maternity home. Fortunately, the majority of such homes open their doors to nonresidents of the urban areas in which the homes are located.

The Value of Case-Work Service

"The art of helping people out of trouble." Case work may be defined as simply as that, in spite of its complexity. But however its skills are described, no one who truly understands them can doubt their value to a woman illegitimately pregnant who must decide whether to face the world with a child born out of wedlock or to give him to someone else. This experience calls for courage of a high order. In this situation above all others, a girl suffers deep fears because she knows the social cruelties that await her. Often she stands alone in her bewilderment. Often she is torn between her wish to be free from the social consequences of her own actions—to escape disgrace for herself and her family—and her responsibility toward the new life she is bearing.

The usual avenues of advice and comfort seem to be or are closed to an unmarried woman who is pregnant. Her circle—family, friends, work associates—may contain individuals who will stand by her, but in her panic how is she to know which ones will respond with help rather than reproach? Her trouble is a test of *their* courage also, as well as of their affection and intelligence. One unmarried mother may feel hesitant about talking to anyone, even a staff member of a social agency. Another may welcome the advice of someone she has not previously known—particularly a professional person with an un-

676781°—46—2

15

blaming attitude toward her and knowledge of how to help her meet her difficulty.

An unmarried mother will accept the help of a case-work agency with greater ease if she has learned through some channel to think of the case worker as a person who "listens thoughtfully and with discernment, without blaming, without judging . . . understands much of human behavior, the forces moving within folks . . . knows their family patterns, their 'folks ways,' believes in the value of human beings, their improvability, their courage to face life as it is." She "cares for people's happiness, their personal satisfactions, but her chief concern is their general social usefulness."[1]

Helping in the situation of illegitimate pregnancy takes skill on the part of the case worker. Nothing about it is simple, involving as it does confused human emotions seldom disciplined by thought. Attitudes toward the young woman who breaks the code of sexual morality have been undergoing a gradual change towards greater tolerance since Victorian days. War produces its own brand of accelerated tolerance that must be considered apart from the general trend. The basic pattern of suffering for the woman, nevertheless, remains much the same. She feels great loneliness—in sharp contrast to a young wife happily married and expecting her first child. The wife is usually surrounded by devoted family and friends who plan enthusiastically for her welfare and for the health and future of the coming baby.

With the pregnant unmarried girl denial and concealment of pregnancy are common. Medical care is postponed. Living arrangements and even food are often perilously different from what she should have. Disgrace threatens her, or she believes it does. Guilt, anxiety, and fear influence her actions.

Attitudes toward illegitimate pregnancy differ, of course, among the young women, their families, and the communities in which they live. Economic conditions, social position, religious background, and the cultural pattern exert their influences. Under these circumstances the girl from the established, well-to-do family may need assistance more than the girl without resources whose unconventional behavior is accepted by her social group. The family of means may be influenced by the fact that it has hard-earned prestige to lose. Its daughter may suffer the severest panic and walk the hardest road.

"The unmarried mother" and the father of her child are far from being a type, a fact that makes the *individual* approach of case work a valuable one. All kinds of human beings are represented and all grades of intelligence. The unmarried father and mother may be school children—or they may be middle aged. One or both parents may be married—a complicating factor in planning for the baby. The friend-

---

[1] So You're Going Into Social Work. Institute of Family Service, Cleveland, Ohio.

16

ships or acquaintanceships that result in illegitimate pregnancy may have been of long or short duration. The man is perhaps well known to the young woman; he may have mentioned marriage. In contrast, his first name may be the only clue to his identity.

CASE WORK ADAPTED TO MATERNITY HOMES

What case work has to offer to the unmarried mother and to the maternity home involves questions of immediate concern to both the mother and the home in addition to questions involving long-time planning for the mother and her baby. The way in which these problems are met will influence the mother's ability to make the most of her maternity-home experience and will influence the future welfare of her baby.

The first contact

Case-work skills are useful from the very beginning of a girl's relationship with the home. The worker can be helpful in handling admissions. It is best for her to interview the young woman, if possible, to help her decide whether care in a maternity home is the most suitable plan for her. Pregnant girls often write in panic for admission. They do not stop to consider their own resources—the possibility, perhaps, of staying with relatives who live in other towns or cities. They do not know of social services other than the maternity home. Besides talking over alternative plans, the worker can tell the young woman in detail the requirements of the home for admission and the regulations for residents, giving her the reasons for them.

Applications from a distance

If the application is made by letter and the distance is too great for a personal call, reaching a decision about admission is much more difficult. Every maternity home will find it helpful to work out some plan for cooperation with case-work agencies elsewhere. These should be carefully chosen with due regard to the confidential nature of the applications. Child-welfare divisions of State departments of welfare and local child-welfare services can frequently be useful when an applicant lives in a rural area.

In a sense, this type of cooperation is an extension of the services of a maternity home itself and can be explained to the unmarried mother on that basis. In writing to ask her permission for a personal interview its advantage to her can be pointed out. Perhaps she would prefer to make the arrangement herself directly with the State office or local agency, it may be suggested. Perhaps she will reply by suggesting an alternative, such as visiting the maternity home in advance of admission.

Immediate and integrated attention

Regardless of whether the application is made by letter or by a personal visit, the maternity home is responsible for seeing that the girl receives immediate assistance, particularly medical care if she is not getting it.

In a city that has a number of agencies giving service to unmarried mothers it is wise to refer an applicant to another agency only after making sure of the agency's willingness to help her. Unless this is done, unmarried mothers are likely to be passed from one agency to another, an experience that may be very destructive. If, after agreeing to accept the girl for service, the agency finds that it cannot do so or if the young woman fails to make a contact with the agency as she agreed to do, the agency will report back in order that another plan may be made. This is extremely important. Young women who are emotionally disturbed about pregnancy are likely to become discouraged by obstacles to obtaining service, and, as a result, to make ill-advised plans that do not sufficiently safeguard the welfare of their babies.

The most opportune time for an expectant mother to discuss her difficulties, to propose the solutions she sees, and to begin working on a way out of her situation is when she is filled with anxiety for herself and the coming baby. It is then that she approaches an agency for help. She is more likely to accept its help instead of shying away from what she considers rigid rules, if agency policies and procedures are kept flexible and receptive.

Continuous service in the home

The time that an unmarried mother spends in a maternity home is only a brief interlude in her total life span. It can, nevertheless, start her on the way to a richer life which she may find through learning to know herself better, being freed from some of her anxieties, and developing new satisfactions. The relationship with the case worker can be one of the strongest factors in her growth experience, if the case worker has been well chosen.

The case worker, it is clear, is responsible for continuous service to the girl while she is living in the maternity home and for as long afterward as service is needed. As a result of several recent studies of unmarried mothers known to social agencies, it is evident that services to unmarried mothers are usually terminated too abruptly—while they still need assistance.

The essence of case work is individualized treatment; that is, helping each unmarried mother in whatever way *she* needs help. The worker considers her as an individual different from all other individuals and with certain inherent strengths and weaknesses. In cooperation with the staff of the maternity home the case worker can do many things to aid the girl's adjustment to the home. After she comes to know her through interviews, the worker can help other staff members to understand the girl's behavior and to plan an effective program for her. Likewise, others working in the home can help the case worker to understand the girl.

Arrangements for interviews

Interviews between the unmarried mother and the case worker should continue as long as the girl remains in the home. Their frequency will depend on the girl's need for service. A girl who has many difficulties and who is obviously disturbed by her pregnancy will undoubtedly require more assistance than the girl who is naturally well adjusted and whose family accepted the fact of her situation in a wholesome way. Many girls will need regular interviews of at least an hour once a week or, perhaps, even oftener. These interviews may be held in the office of the case worker employed by the home or, if the services are provided by another agency, the interviews may take place in the agency's office.

This latter plan has certain advantages in that the girl can take responsibility for her appointments and has an opportunity to be away from the home. She may feel more at ease and be freer to discuss her problems if the appointments are not at the maternity home. Wherever the interviews are held, however, privacy is essential and also surroundings that will make the unmarried mother feel comfortably at ease.

The interviews

Interviews with the unmarried mother will begin on the subjects uppermost in her mind. The case worker, by an understanding, uncensorious, and objective attitude, will encourage the mother to discuss her difficulties and the solutions that seem possible to her. Out of the case worker's wealth of experience in dealing with similar situations, she will know when to interject a comment that will lead the girl into further exploration of her problem. The worker will know the implications of what is said and of the way it is expressed and also the significance of what is left unsaid. Through the interviews a young woman who has been deprived of emotional satisfactions and is in conflict with herself and others loses much of her hostility and is freed to go ahead with constructive plans for the present and future.

Many unmarried mothers have met with deprivation throughout their lives and have missed a warm affectional relationship with their own parents. They want to talk about their past experiences, what life has done to them, how they feel toward their parents and brothers and sisters, and how pregnancy without marriage will change their lives.

One girl's profit.—The conflict of Jean R. with herself and everyone else illustrates these points. Soon after the attractive, 19-year-old girl entered a maternity home she made herself disliked. She provoked quarrels with other girls, objected to work, and demanded special favors. Jean resisted vigorously when she learned that all residents were expected to see the case worker. She went sullenly to the first interview. To her surprise, however, she liked the worker. Later Jean did learn to use the interviews to discuss her difficulties. Just before she left the home she talked about her early resistance. "I didn't want to confide in anyone," she said, "I just wouldn't have anyone prying around. You didn't pry. You helped *me* to talk. No matter how mean I was or what I told you, you never held anything against me. You trusted me—*always.*"

What had caused Jean's conflicts came out in the interviews, gradually. She had known insecurity early. Her parents were divorced when she was 4. The father, whom Jean loved deeply, won custody of the children. But he put them separately in the homes of different relatives, all of whom were reluctant to take them. The father and mother moved from place to place, seldom seeing their children. At the time the mother married her third husband, Jean was 16. Suddenly her mother appeared to take her to the distant home of the new husband. On the trip she forbade her daughter to call her "mother." "That was a big joke on me," said Jean in telling about it, "all I ever wanted was a real home and a chance to talk to the kids in the block about 'mother and dad.'" Her mother kept her only 3 months.

Step by step in the talks Jean learned that the lack of stability and affection in her childhood had made it hard for her to be friendly. The case worker helped her to master an intense fear of death in childbirth and to sort out her mixed feelings about her unborn baby.

Jean hoped for a daughter, saying, "I'll do better by my little girl than my mother did by me." But Jean didn't have that chance, because her baby died at birth. Could she have done a good job as an only parent? First she had to learn to live at peace with herself. For that she had made a good beginning.

Relationships.—The case worker will probably have an opportunity to meet some members of the girl's family during her stay in the maternity home and to discuss with them future plans for the mother and baby. This should not be done, however, without the young woman's permission unless she is obviously unable to handle the situation. Even then, it is to be hoped that she will eventually see the advantage of sharing her experience with her own people—providing it is advantageous. How important it is for the case worker to discuss the situation with members of the family depends upon their attitude toward the mother and baby and her attitude toward them.

Sooner or later the unmarried mother will want to talk to the case worker about her relationship with, and feeling toward, the father of the baby. This attitude will influence in no small part her attitude toward the baby and her adjustment to the maternity home. Frequently the attitude the unmarried mother expresses at first toward the father of her coming child is not her true feeling for him but only a "cover up" for her pent-up emotion of hurt pride or is what she thinks is expected of her. The same is true of her expression of feeling for the baby. It is helpful, therefore, to give her the opportunity to discuss with the case worker this relationship with the father in order to settle her own conflicts about it as well as to decide on the responsibility she would like him to assume.

The unmarried mother may also want the case worker to talk to the father of the child in regard to his attitude toward her and the baby. If he acknowledges his responsibility and if real affection exists between them, he will no doubt continue to see the girl at the maternity home. If she has failed in her own efforts to reach a satisfactory agreement with him, she may want the worker to interview him as often as necessary. He, too, may be in need of case-work assistance. In some instances it may be wise for the same case worker to talk with both the young woman and the man but in others a different worker may be advisable. It is important to remember that if the baby is to be placed in adoption details about the father's background are as significant as details about the mother's.

Many unmarried mothers, in contrast to those just mentioned, are inclined to give a fictitious story about the man and to deny knowledge of who or where he is. They do this for a variety of reasons, frequently because the case worker has expected the mother to discuss this matter too soon, before she has learned to know or trust the worker. Perhaps the girl has not told the man of the coming baby or is dissatisfied with his attitude. In this latter instance, she may want the case worker to interview him. Whatever her plan, the case worker's job is to assist her in thinking it through. Interviews with the man may lead to a voluntary acknowledgment of paternity and contributions to the maintenance of the child or to a decision by the mother to take court action. The case worker then has much responsibility in preparing the mother for interviews in connection with the court proceedings.

Many questions.—In addition to the emotional problems that confront the unmarried mother other realistic issues arise on which the case worker can give help. No one is in a better position to put at the girl's disposal the resources of the community—cultural, educational, religious, or recreational—that will broaden her horizon. The stay in the maternity home offers the case worker a chance to advise the young woman who has not had employment about vocational opportunities and help her plan her training either while she is in the home or after she leaves. When the girl is ready to leave, the case worker can help her find a job suited to her ability and interests.

The unmarried mother may need assistance in finding a place to live or she may need foster-home care for the child. She may need financial assistance to tide her over until she has sufficient funds for her own maintenance. Regardless of what she decides to do, a crucial adjustment faces her when she leaves the maternity home. The social worker can prepare her for this in many ways and during the early months of adjustment can stand by to respond to any need. The stay in the maternity home should have given the girl a new perspective on life, new interests, courage to face the future, and more ability to handle her own life.

THE DECISION—TO KEEP OR TO RELINQUISH THE CHILD

"What shall I do with my baby?" is the question uppermost in the minds of most women who are illegitimately pregnant. The question cannot be answered at once, however, as the reply depends on many complex factors that must be weighed. The factors are different for each mother. They grow out of the kind of person she is, her relationships, what her life has been so far, and what she is likely to make of her future—particularly what kind of mother she would be under the most difficult circumstances for motherhood. These pages now present some of the factors a resident of a maternity home should consider, with good counsel at hand, before deciding this important question.

Perhaps the young woman and her family already have a plan formulated when she arrives at the home, made by thoughtful consideration or, may be, in panic. On arrival a girl may express indecision and desperation or she may be too fearful of being considered a "bad mother" to put her feelings into words. She may be told that because the birth is not imminent the matter will not be discussed until later. She may be led to believe, not told in so many words, that a "good mother" keeps her child or she may be reminded that one condition for admission is that babies be breast fed for 6 weeks or 3 months. Perhaps she is told that other girls have shown similar concern but learned to love their babies and have decided to keep them. Assurance may be given that the case worker will help her make a plan and that discussion can start immediately. In some instances adoption may be mentioned.

Many maternity homes expect the girl who accepts their care to keep her child. The original purpose of holding inflexibly to this principle was commendable. It was a recognition by those responsible for maternity homes of the moral obligation of a mother toward her child and an expression of their desire to win more tolerance for unmarried mothers so that they could bring up their children under favorable circumstances. The homes believed that the mother had a right to keep her child and that the child had a right to remain with his kin. Many believed that the child would have a stabilizing effect on the mother. Too little thought was given to such questions as whether the mother was prepared to keep her child; what she had to offer him as a parent; whether she could support him; or whether she could face the many difficulties that would confront her with a child born out of wedlock. She was given good physical care in the maternity home but was allowed to go away with little preparation for the realities she would meet when she stepped out of the door with a fatherless baby in her arms.

Freedom of choice

Current philosophy among case workers and representatives of maternity homes coincides on some of these points, certainly on the need for greater tolerance and understanding. The girl who wants to keep her child and who sees the way clear to do so should be helped to make such a plan feasible. Return to her family is possible in some instances, with support assured. Other mothers will require economic assistance at least temporarily and may obtain it from either public or private social agencies. Fortunately, aid to dependent children may be given under the Social Security Act regardless of status of birth, which means that many unmarried mothers are receiving this form of assistance for their children. As aid to dependent children is a State program, eligibility requirements and the amount of assistance differ from State to State because they are based upon State law and the policies, rules, and regulations of the administering agency. Unwise discrimination against unmarried mothers persists in some communities because of the fear that financial help would encourage illegitimacy. Unfortunately, too, in many instances enough case-work service does not accompany financial aid.

Everyone tends to oversimplify the decision the mother has to make: to keep or not to keep her child. The relationship of the mother and child is far more complex than appears on the surface and the decisions made at the beginning of the relationship influence profoundly not only the mother's life but the entire future of the child. Whoever attempts to help the mother make her plans should possess the best skills known to social work. Few studies have been made on this mother-child relationship but the records of case-work agencies might reveal many experiences, some happy, some tragic, that could be utilized as a basis for more scientific, objective action.

Adjustments to be faced

Whatever the mother's decision about her child's future she is likely to find herself in a very different position from that of the married woman with a new baby. The universal first question, "What is going to happen to my baby?" shows that the idea of separation is present from the beginning. During the stay in the maternity home, the nurse usually has far more responsibility for the baby than the mother has. If the mother returns to her parental home, she may have to share the child with the grandparents to a far greater degree than the usual child of legitimate birth is shared. This may be for any of several reasons: The home is the grandparents' and they may be helping to support the mother and child; they may mistrust their daughter's ability to care for the child because of her extreme youth or they may question her judgment because she has had a child out of wedlock; by assuming the responsibility for the baby they may wish to shield their daughter's reputation from prying new acquaintances or to give her time to reestablish her social life; the grandmother usually takes care of the baby while the mother works; and the grandfather feels that he should play a father's part in the life of his fatherless grandchild. If the child is placed in foster care, the responsibility for its care rests largely with the foster mother or with the staff of the institution. The unmarried mother must adjust to a second place in which she does not have the opportunity of doing many things that are normally considered the mother's right.

This is only one of the many adjustments the unmarried mother must make in relation to her child. Too frequently she must be prepared to struggle for the child's support—stretching the small earnings meant for one to pay the living expenses of herself and her baby. Expressions of sympathy for her are seldom heard, although almost everyone laments, and justly so, the struggle that lies ahead for the young widow with one child or for the "war widow." In most instances the widow's lot is far easier than the unmarried mother's, because her plight may bring help instead of hostility.

24

Of her own volition or on the insistence of her family or public official—if she applies for relief—the unmarried mother may initiate proceedings to obtain support from the father of her child. In all probability she assumes that the amount will be sufficient for the baby's maintenance. In reality, we know from such studies as have been made that support from the father is at best pitiably small and that the amount contributed is usually larger during the first few years of the child's life than later when expenses for the child are greater. Other means must be found to supplement this support.

Many of the mothers who have been known to social agencies have not had vocational training and are doing work that requires little training, if any. If the mother is in a skilled occupation such as nursing, teaching, or social work she may find that she is unable to continue in this occupation because of her illegitimate pregnancy and later because of her child. She may have to seek employment in a new field at a lower salary. Support for herself may be difficult and may leave no margin for the care of her child.

An unmarried mother may have to forego her former recreational and leisure-time activities. She is expected by family, friends, and community to tread the straight and narrow path and to demonstrate that she has "learned her lesson." Sometimes she is expected to forsake the usual pleasures of youth and the companionship of men. In many subtle ways she is even now expected to wear the "scarlet letter." The more she does for the child and denies herself just ordinary fun, the greater the approval she receives from society.

The child's welfare

In view of the many adjustments that the unmarried mother will have to make when she leaves the maternity home, she should have the most skilled help available in the community in planning for her child. His welfare is paramount. Protection for the child can best be afforded through good case-work services to the mother. Consideration of the plans for the child should start as soon as feasible—preferably during early pregnancy before the mother enters the maternity home. In any event, this vital subject should be a part of her interviews with the case worker as soon as the young woman is known to the home. She may bring up the subject herself or the case worker may have to introduce it. To discuss the subject early is a far sounder policy than to tell a girl who is troubled about plans for the baby that the subject cannot be discussed, or at least that no decision can be made until after the birth of the baby. The matter is of such vital concern to the mother that preventing her from talking about it may impede her whole adjustment and block the opportunity for her to work off some of her anxiety and hostility.

25

Superintendents of maternity homes and case workers frequently fear to allow girls to discuss plans early, in the belief that the girls may make decisions that they will later regret because during pregnancy they may not be in emotional or physical condition to think clearly. These superintendents and case workers may put off the decision in the hope that once the mother has seen her baby, maternal affection will prevent separation. Furthermore, they know from experience with other mothers and other babies that the child may be found unsuitable for adoption; in that event, a plan for adoption formulated early would have to be set aside.

Although the purpose of interviews on this subject is to help the mother arrive at a workable plan for the child, the plan that she makes early in pregnancy may not be the plan she ultimately carries out. She will be in a better position, however, to make a final decision if she has ample opportunity for discussion and thought.

Responses of mothers to planning

Unmarried mothers respond to the necessity for decision in accordance with the degree of their adjustment to life. Some, who are well integrated persons, whatever their age, will face their difficult situation squarely and will decide quite objectively whether to keep or to relinquish their babies. Others, neurotic individuals who have suffered much deprivation in childhood and who are emotionally immature and unstable, may appear to be just as sure of their decisions. Some may be determined to keep their babies, saying, "It's my baby and no one shall have it." But to those who understand human behavior, it will be evident that such an individual may not really be prepared to accept the responsibility nor really desire to do so.

WHEN THE MOTHER KEEPS HER BABY

Many unmarried mothers take it for granted from the beginning that they will keep their babies, believing this course inevitable. This decision should be arrived at as thoughtfully as the decision to place the child in adoption. Unfortunately, this is not always done. Too often the plan is made as the easiest way out of the situation for the social agency. The mother, knowing of no alternatives, agrees. If case workers are truly interested in preventing an unhappy life experience for the mother and child growing out of the fact of illegitimate birth, more careful study than is now being given should be concentrated on plans for the unmarried mother who leaves the maternity home with her child.

26

Is her plan a workable one? Will support for the child be adequate? Will the home afford security and affection and a chance for growth and normal development?

In her parent's home

These assurances are as important for the child returning to the mother's parental home as for the child of a girl who lives in her own apartment. We have been too free in assuming that relatives' homes are a satisfactory solution, and we forget that many young women who are unmarried mothers have been in serious conflict with their parents. Some unmarried mothers are themselves of illegitimate birth. Yet the baby returns with the mother to the environment in which the original difficulty developed—perhaps later to follow in the mother's footsteps.

Often social workers have no alternative but to let the mother go to her home because of lack of resources. If so, the plan can be carried out with some awareness of what is likely to happen. The mother can be prepared for some of the attitudes and some of the problems she will encounter and she may be given sustaining help over a period of years, if she wishes it. The child in the parental home, or elsewhere, should be thought of not merely as an infant but as a growing child who may have many difficulties to face because of his illegitimate birth.

In a foster home

Some mothers who keep their babies will not be able to return to the parental home but will need foster care for their babies. Such placement service needs to be available to every maternity home through a qualified child-placing agency or child-welfare worker. If the mother cannot pay for boarding care, another source of funds is necessary. Foster homes for the babies of unmarried mothers have to be selected even more carefully than the usual boarding home. Their supervision by a social agency is essential.

In addition to giving adequate care to the baby, the foster parents, if they are willing, can provide a "home" for the mother when she has free time to visit her child. They will be chosen because they are persons who accept the mother, that is, have wholesome, friendly regard for her and feel no need to punish her for her sex behavior. Ideally, the foster parents are so secure in their relationships that they will not need to supplant the mother as the real parent. They can learn to distinguish between the kind of assistance they can best give the mother and the service given by the case worker.

A type of plan that has been used effectively is the foster home in which the mother and baby can live together. The foster mother assumes full responsibility for the child while the mother is at work. Agreements about the details of care need to be reached before the placement is made, such as the amount of responsibility the mother will assume when she is at home, and which of the two will prepare the child's food on Sunday and do the baby's laundry. Unless such matters are discussed in advance and unless the foster mother and the child's mother accept the plan whole-heartedly, friction is likely to result.

Many an unmarried mother cannot make up her mind about keeping her baby at first and may wish to have him placed for a while. The mother may request placement in a home with the baby or foster care for the child apart from her. This latter plan may afford her greater opportunity to learn whether she is willing to make the many adjustments that lie ahead for her if she keeps her baby. If she lives with the baby, separation may become too difficult even though she does not really want responsibility for his care.

Child-placing agencies and children's institutions have had a great deal of experience with unmarried mothers who place their children in foster care. Some mothers may take little responsibility for their children's support, or visit them irregularly, or give them little real affection. Other mothers, particularly those whose children are placed in family homes, may shower attention on them but in a way that makes matters difficult for the foster mothers. Such behavior may be an indication of an immature, self-centered individual who has no real interest in her child.

The child is caught between conflicting disciplines and receives no consistent affection or security from the mother. Owing to the difficulties the mother causes in a foster home, the child is likely to be moved from one home to another. This situation may continue year after year with the mother refusing to make any other plan for her child. Perhaps this condition drags on until the child is beyond the age for placement in adoption.

Many such children spend their lives in institutions or in a series of foster homes, making no real attachments to anyone. One such child at 10 years of age is a disturbed, bewildered boy with many behavior problems. He has lived in 20 foster homes. At the time of his birth his mother was a docile, receptive girl who agreed with the philosophy of the maternity home that she should keep her baby. Her parents refused to allow her to live at home if she kept him. She went to work in a store, paid the child's board regularly, and visited him in the foster home every 2 weeks. Gradually, however, her payments stopped. Twice she attempted suicide. Either the original plan was an unsuitable one for both her and the child, or the mother was not given enough case-work assistance in carrying out the plan.

Another mother now says that maybe it was a mistake for her to have kept her child. She has been extremely possessive of him, yet in many ways she has shown hostility toward him. At 6 years of age he presents many problems. He has lived in 26 foster homes—some found by the mother and some by social agencies.

Another mother is loud in her complaints against every agency that has tried to help her. She makes unfounded complaints against the foster mothers and refuses to contribute to the child's maintenance. This procedure has gone on for 8 years to the detriment of a child of superior intelligence. Children who go through these experiences have no opportunity to establish a love relationship with a parent or a parent substitute. Gaining security from being in any one home long enough to get the feeling of belonging there is denied them. They are "pillar to post" children.

Review of the plan

Child-placement agencies have become much more conscious of these unsatisfactory situations in recent years. Some agencies now tell the mother that they will care for the baby until a certain date, at which time the whole plan will be reviewed with her. In this way she knows that she is expected to work on the solution of the problem—what is best to do about her child—with the aid of the case worker.

The purpose of the review is to study further the mother's relationship with the child to determine whether she is interested in him and to gage the sustaining quality of what interest she may have and her ability to bring up the child in a satisfactory manner. One author has suggested a list of points that may be used in evaluating an unmarried mother's interest in her child. They are as follows:[2]

1. *A time limit:* Will she agree to a temporary placement with an appraisal of the plan at the end of 6 months?

2. *Scale of payment:* What proportion of her earnings does she volunteer for the child's support?

3. *Visits to her baby:* Does she visit regularly? How long does she stay? Is her time spent with the child or with others in the foster family? When did she first begin to absent herself from the child?

4. *Gifts to her child:* Does she give her child clothing? Is it appropriate or inappropriate? Does she give harmful toys, or does she refrain from ever giving him a gift?

5. *Behavior toward her child:* How does she play with him?

[2] Case Work Service for Unmarried Mothers, by Ruth F. Brenner. The Family, vol. 22, Nov.-Dec., 1941, pp. 211–219 and 269–276. Family Welfare Association of America, 130 E. 22 St., New York 10, N. Y.

What does she do with him? Is she gentle and tender, or rough in her handling of him?

6. *Her expectations:* What does she want from her child? How much response? More of an adult response than would be normal for a youngster of her child's age?

7. *Her fantasies about her child:* Does she see him as her protector in a few years or as a source of support for herself?

8. *Excursions:* What visiting does she do with her child? Whom does she take him to see? Or does she never take him out? What recreational trips does she take him on?

9. *Discussions about her child:* With whom does she talk about her child? With others besides the case worker? With foster mother, foster father, her own parents, her siblings, her baby's father, her friends, her employer? Or does she tell no one of her child and confine her talk of him to the case worker?

10. *Anxieties regarding her child:* Does she worry about supporting him or about his name, particularly when entering school, or how he will feel toward her when he discovers that his birth was illegitimate? Does she question the adequacy of care given by his foster parents?

11. *Interrelationship of mother, foster mother, and child:* Can the mother share possession of her child with foster parents? Does she quarrel with foster parents over the care of the child? Does she attempt to precipitate quarrels between the foster parents?

When the mother marries

Marriage of the parents in order to give the baby a name was the solution formerly in vogue. It was not always accomplished, of course, but the family of the young woman usually tried to bring it about if they saw any possibility of doing so, often using every kind of pressure. The custom still persists to a more limited degree, sometimes with the planned intent to take advantage of increasingly liberalized divorce laws after the birth has been legitimatized.

When the advice of case workers is sought, marriage of the natural parents is only one of the solutions considered and then only when a real basis for marriage exists. If there is such a basis, of course it is the logical solution. But case workers realize that without this foundation marriage can bring little but unhappiness for mother, father, and child. These marriages, in fact, need a particularly strong foundation, as factors inherent in the original situation may easily wreck the union.

No information is available on the number of unmarried mothers who marry someone other than the father of the child, nor do we have sufficient information to know how such a plan succeeds for the child. The situation involves the usual adjustments of a stepparent relationship added to those growing out of illegitimate birth. Is the stepfather objective enough about the situation so that the child will have the love and security he needs? Is he tolerant of the child's misbehavior or is he oversevere with him because of the thought of the other man? When children are born of this marriage, is the child of illegitimate birth treated with the same consideration and affection as the other children? Does the sight of the child put doubt in the stepfather's mind about the faithfulness of his wife to him and so create an atmosphere of conflict in the home?

Case workers and others have looked upon such marriages as a fortunate solution for the unmarried mother and her baby, and in many instances they may be. Partly because the girl wants to forget the past and partly because case workers are busy people, case-work services are often terminated as soon as marriage seems imminent. In some instances this may be the time that case work is needed most—to help the couple make a success of their marriage and to insure wholesome development of the child.

Some of the difficulties that a case worker might assist in preventing are shown in the marriage of Anna L., a girl who had immigrated to the United States alone. Anna had not been here long when she became pregnant. She had a few friends but because she had no relatives to help her she chose to be cared for in a maternity home. As soon as she could go to work again her infant son was placed in an institution. He remained there for 4 years and was then cared for in a series of foster homes. Anna supported her child and visited him regularly. When the boy was about 6 years of age she married a man who had been her friend for some time. He had known the child, had taken him on trips, had given him gifts, and in every way had demonstrated affection for him. The boy was devoted to both his mother and his new father. The family, to the delight of their friends, built a small home and moved to the country.

Gradually the difficulties began. Anna told her friends that she wanted to work so that her husband would not need to contribute so much for her child's support. Later she said that she had lost her feeling for the boy. She felt cold toward him: she had no patience with him. She explained that her husband was jealous of the child and hurt her by his remarks about her early experience. She did not want to give up her home, she said, but began to consider giving up her son.

The child was a well adjusted, friendly, happy boy giving every promise of normal development. Children and adults were enthusiastic about him. Then he began to steal—little things that he would use at school as gifts to the other children. The stepfather insisted that the mother search the child's pockets before he left for school and kept telling the lad that "he would land in the reform school." The only solution Anna could see was to place her son in adoption.

Would this solve Anna's problem? Probably not. It certainly would not solve the boy's, as by this time he had reached an age at which it is difficult, though not impossible, to find an adoptive home. The scars left from feeling unwanted and unloved and from being told, perhaps, that he was a "bastard child" can never be erased. The hurt will penetrate deeper when he realizes that he is forsaken by his mother who plans to give him to someone else. He seems caught in a tragic net. Skillful handling of the first signs of disunion—requiring greater knowledge than the mother had—might have kept the home a good place for the boy.

PLACEMENT OF THE RELINQUISHED CHILD

The waiting period

The girl who decides to give up her child has a right to know from the case worker how placement will be made, that is, what procedure will be followed to insure a good home for the baby. She may relinquish her parental rights to a child-placing agency in the community as soon as she fully decides on this step. In some instances relinquishment will occur soon after the child's birth, especially when the case worker has known the mother through much of her pregnancy and the two have talked over thoroughly the mother's wish for the adoption of the child. The baby can then be placed in a boarding home for further study, awaiting placement in an adoptive home. Support for the child may be contributed by the mother or her family or it may be wise for the agency to pay the full amount.

Some psychiatrists and case workers in child-placing agencies recommend early placement of infants for adoption. They base their recommendations on evidence showing that infants thrive best when mothered by one person. The fewer times the infant is placed, they believe, the better for his physical and emotional development. When adoption is clearly indicated as the best plan, these specialists recommend an observation period in a foster family home where board is paid until adoption can be safely and wisely arranged, possibly at 4 months of age. When a baby is about 6 months old he usually establishes his relationship to the person who cares for him. Greater caution is required, however, in early placements for adoption than in later ones, because a baby's potential development is more difficult to appraise than that of an older child.

During the observation period the mother may change her mind and decide to keep the child if she sees her way clear to do so. She should realize, however, that once she signs the final papers giving up her parental rights in the child, she has no further responsibility for or right to him or to be consulted on plans for him.

Maternity homes are not licensed usually as child-placing agencies. When adoption is indicated, the best agency in the community responsible for the placement of children is the one to use.

Unsuitability for adoption

There are a variety of reasons why a child may be unsuitable for adoption. Such children sometimes present problems that are very complex and involve continuous study, long-time planning, and a considerable expenditure of funds. To give these children protection, child-placing agencies need to have flexible policies for unmarried mothers and their children and to use this flexibility from the very beginning of the service.

For example, a 16-year-old girl was sent by her family to an aunt in another State when pregnancy was discovered. Social conditions were so deplorable in the milltown where she grew up that her return there seemed unwise. There young people had no wholesome recreation, no proper schooling, and no social protection. Before the baby's birth the aunt consulted a children's agency about having the child placed in adoption soon after birth. She refused the agency's assistance, however, when she was told that her niece would be sent to a maternity home and would be required to remain there with the baby for 6 months. The aunt, discouraged by this inflexible policy, turned to a well known physician who agreed to give the girl prenatal care, to deliver her in a private hospital, and to place the child in adoption. He carried out the plan without knowing that mental tests had revealed the girl was subnormal mentally or that nothing was known of the father of the baby. Obviously a child-placing agency could have made a far safer plan for the child and for the adoptive parents. Rigidity of policy in the beginning defeated the protection that was the agency's goal.

The storm center

Families sometimes make a decision about the future of the baby that is in direct opposition to the wishes of the mother and that brings about a disastrous plan or lack of plan for her child. The mother may decide to keep her baby although her family insists upon adoption.

The reasons for such differences of opinion are many. Parents perhaps consider that the presence of a child will jeopardize the girl's whole future or that she is too young for such responsibility. The baby may be used as a means of punishment, that is, the parents may wish to deprive their daughter of her child to punish her or the daughter may wish to keep her child to further offend her parents with whom she is in conflict.

For example, the daughter of parents in good circumstances, a 16-year-old girl, became pregnant by a boy a year older, whom she wanted to marry. Her parents refused to allow this marriage. She had been "running around" against the wishes of her parents who were greatly disturbed by their loss of control over her. The mother sought the help of a social agency but by refusing to permit more than one interview with her daughter prevented anything constructive from being done. The mother told her daughter—falsely—that the social agency wanted to place her in a correctional school, which was in reality the plan the mother desired. The daughter was so incensed by her mother's treatment of her that she refused to consider giving up her child and was barred from her home because she kept him. When the baby was 6 months old the girl was found sitting at a table in a roadhouse with the sick child in her lap. She said then that prostitution would be the easiest way for her to earn her living.

An 18-year-old girl came from a well-to-do family. On the surface she would appear to have everything that an adolescent girl could desire—attentive parents, a good home, friends, fun, and fine educational opportunities. In reality she had a mother who dominated her whole life, who treated her as a little girl, trying to prevent her from having friends. When the mother discovered her daughter's pregnancy she would not let her see the father of her unborn child. It was the mother who made all decisions for her daughter and for the future of the coming baby. If the baby stayed in that home, he would be in the steady cross-fire of conflict between mother and daughter. His chance for a normal life would be greater with well-chosen adoptive parents.

Separation at birth

Separation at birth is contrary to the principles of many maternity homes even if the mother, after careful consideration, wants to surrender custody of her child without seeing him. Those in charge of the home hesitate to put such a plan into practice, fearing that the mother may regret her decision later. They also question the effect on the other residents of the home, believing that learning of the possibility might increase the number who request this solution of their difficulties.

For the mother to give up her child without seeing him is a plan that should be made only after careful consideration of all the factors in the situation. If, however, the mother has had good case-work service over a long enough period or if she insists upon placement in adoption without seeing the child, the case worker may agree with the mother that separation at birth is the most suitable plan for her and her baby. The traumatic effect of giving up her baby may be less severe for her if she never sees him. In such instances maternity homes should plan carefully to protect the mother from unnecessary strain and confusion.

Must the mother nurse her child?

The question of early separation of mother and baby is closely related to the policy of maternity homes in regard to the nursing of the infant by the mother. Here also the individual approach is important. Nevertheless, many homes state in their requirements for admission that the mother must nurse the child for a minimum period, some of them for as little as 3 weeks, if she is physically able to do so. The basis of this requirement is the belief that for physical and perhaps emotional reasons every mother should nurse her child and the established fact that a child who is breast fed has a better start in life. Exceptions to this rule are rarely made even though the situation of the mother seems to warrant it. Another practice that does not allow for individual choice is the practice in a few homes of drying up the milk of all mothers immediately after delivery.

Actually, it would be well if exactly the same advice about nursing her baby could be given to an unmarried mother as is given to one who is married. Even with married mothers, health and social situations may arise in which the physician recommends artificial feeding of the infant. Three differences have to be considered, however, that make immediate artificial feeding more often necessary for the unmarried mother—the possibility of early separation of mother and child in adoption; the frequent need of the unmarried girl to return to work at once; and the danger that the mother required to nurse the child against her wishes or her considered judgment may interpret it as punishment and develop emotional difficulties that may harm her and her child. Her objection, if she is about to relinquish him, may be sound.

Whatever is said about the advantages of breast feeding is best stated scientifically and objectively as accepted medical fact, during the talks given to the residents on health care for mother and child. The young women will understand, then, that they are getting the same information that is given to all mothers and are expected to nurse their babies, if it is possible, for the same health reasons. Conversely, as a private obstetrician makes exceptions, for certain patients, to his own customary advice about nursing, some exceptions can be made for mothers in a maternity home. The mother who has thoughtfully decided on relinquishment and who fears to become too attached to her baby need not be required to nurse him for a few weeks but can be assured that artificial feeding will be safe for her baby if done under the care of a pediatrician.

WAYS OF PROVIDING CASE-WORK SERVICE

The discussion so far has attempted to show in some measure what case work has to offer to unmarried mothers who go to maternity homes for care. Some homes provide this service. Among those that do not, many recognize its value and, ideally, want to add it to their program. Practically, however, they ask how this can be done, in short, which of several methods of providing case-work service is the most practicable for a particular maternity home? Because the answer depends on many factors, each home will want to work out the plan that suits it best. Among the factors to be considered are the type and size of the home, the funds available for staff, the educational and vocational background of the superintendent, the type and quality of the local case-work agencies, and the current supply of qualified case workers. The advantages and disadvantages of several ways of providing case-work service will be considered at this point.

A case worker on the staff

Some maternity homes employ their own case workers. This is a basically sound administrative procedure that is used by other types of institutions. The experience of institutions for children that have for many years tried both plans—having their own case worker or getting this service through another agency—has demonstrated that, in general, case work is more likely to be an integral part of the whole program if the case worker is employed by the institution.

Some of the other advantages are more specific. For example, the case worker is more likely to be fully accepted by the board of directors and staff members under this plan; the case worker who is on the staff can help the nurse or the cook to understand individual girls when questions arise; she is more readily within reach of the residents in the home than an outside worker; the young women feel free to talk to her and to consult her as often as is necessary. Such a worker, provided she has sound professional education and qualifying experience, becomes a specialist in this particular field. This results in excellent service to the individual mothers and leadership to the board of directors and other interested laymen. It may mean continuous service to

36

the unmarried mother from the time she applies for entrance to the maternity home until she no longer has need of assistance or until the responsibility has passed to another agency. It is sometimes best, however, to have the case-work agency that refers a girl to a home continue to work with her while she is there as well as afterward.

The case worker employed by a maternity home is administratively responsible to the superintendent. These two should work in close cooperation for the welfare of the mothers and babies. The duties of each one will, of course, be clearly defined. Matters pertaining to the operation of the home and the total program are the logical responsibility of the superintendent, but policies and procedures for carrying them out may well be formulated in consultation with the case worker because of their emotional and social implications and because of the contribution that the case worker is equipped to make to the various phases of the program. Although she should work in close cooperation with the superintendent and the board of directors who are responsible to the community for the operation of the home, she should be free to exercise her best professional judgment on matters that are distinctly in her field.

Having the case worker on the staff of the maternity home has, however, some disadvantages. Well-qualified case workers are scarce at any time and they are particularly hard to find during a national crisis such as economic depression or war. A family agency or a children's agency with a sizable staff is perhaps in a better position to compete for workers than is a maternity home employing only one case worker. The lone case worker in an institution, whatever the type, is more likely to feel isolated. Close contacts with colleagues mean much to her professional development, particularly if she is young. Shut off from supervision and day-by-day association with other social workers, she has to find other ways of keeping "on her toes." Possibly in these situations supervision by a case-work agency might be arranged.

To the directors of many maternity homes the cost of employing a case worker is undoubtedly an obstacle. Many maternity homes are inadequately financed. The salary of a case worker seems high, perhaps, in comparison with the amount the home has been paying the superintendent. The home cares for relatively few unmarried mothers in the course of a year and the board realizes that the addition of a case worker will raise the per capita cost considerably. This question of whether the increase is justifiable has only one answer—that case-work service is an essential part of the program and should be financed accordingly. Maternity homes that employ their own case workers should have the best qualified workers obtainable as to personality, professional education, and case-work skill.

Because of some of the difficulties mentioned and because of the lack of clear-cut understanding on the qualifications of a case worker, maternity homes, unfortunately, have sometimes employed individuals who are not equipped by education and experience to give the high type of service called for.

Services from outside

Some maternity homes choose to obtain case-work service from another agency rather than to employ their own case worker because of the difficulties already discussed or because of conditions existing in their own communities. This plan frequently works well, particularly if the board of directors and staff of the home are convinced of the value of such an arrangement and if the cooperating family or children's agency accepts the plan wholeheartedly and is prepared to give adequate service.

One of the advantages of outside service is that any case-work agency providing service to families or to children can offer continuous service for the whole period, before the young woman enters the home, during her residence in the home, and after she leaves. Thus the young woman will not need to make adjustments to several agencies. This is particularly important to the unmarried mother who is emotionally disturbed or who hesitates to discuss her problems with more than one individual. Another advantage based on continuous service without referral is that agencies providing service to families are more likely to have funds available for financial assistance if the mother needs it and agencies providing service to children will probably be able to place the baby in a foster home if that is indicated.

The joint plan between home and case-work agency presupposes a willingness on the part of the agency to give service to unmarried mothers who are not residents of the area to which the family or children's agency ordinarily limits its service. Unless such an agreement can be made, another case-work agency must be found to help nonresident mothers. Otherwise the maternity home will have to give up the idea of a cooperative arrangement and employ its own case worker in order to offer a complete service.

If case-work service is provided from outside the home a close working relationship between the maternity home and the agency is essential. Without complete confidence in each other, sharing of information, and joint planning on behalf of the mother and baby, the plan is apt to be ineffective. One way to develop a good relationship is to have the superintendent of the maternity home regularly attend staff meetings of the agency that provides the case-work service. Another is for the agency to arrange for one staff member to give service to the home continuously and so come to know the work thoroughly rather than to assign several workers to the home.

A central service

In some large cities the case-work agencies that serve unmarried mothers have agreed to have one of the agencies serve as a center to which any unmarried mother may be referred. This agency assumes leadership in promoting services, in making known the needs of mothers and their babies, and in keeping the public informed as to how any individual—relative, friend, physician, nurse, teacher, clergyman, employer—may obtain skilled assistance for a pregnant unmarried girl. Research on the subject of illegitimate birth is another part of the central agency's program.

The advantages of a centralized service are obvious. For the girl, centralization eliminates the undesirable passing along from one agency to another at the time of application—one of the greatest faults of service to unmarried mothers. For a friend or relative who knows vaguely that advice can be obtained for a pregnant girl and wants to get it for her quickly, a central agency is a boon, eliminating the confusing choice between agencies. Physicians do not need to know or to attempt to remember which social agency gives which type of service to girls who may come to them for medical care but who need other kinds of care as well. This convenience may easily increase the number of unmarried mothers who go to case-work agencies for help.

Centralization does not mean that one agency alone provides service to unmarried mothers. Other agencies may continue to give assistance to girls who apply directly to them. Moreover, the central agency may interview a girl only briefly before referring her, with her permission, to one of the other agencies. Likewise, it may suggest to a physician inquiring about service for an unmarried mother that because this particular individual could be served best by another agency he arrange for her care there.

A central agency for unmarried mothers, the Women's Service Division of the United Charities, has been in operation in Chicago since early in 1944. It was set up as the result of a study made by the Council of Social Agencies of services for unmarried mothers. This comprehensive, specialized program gives direct service to the mother, coordinates all other services for her, gives information to individuals in answer to specific questions and to the general public through widely read media, and promotes standards and legislation on the subject of illegitimate birth. A central office and four district offices cover the whole city for referral and treatment.

As a private agency supported by the community as a whole, this designated center does not, of course, assume responsibility for all unmarried mothers who seek help from social agencies. Some unmarried mothers may choose other agencies.

A central organization is most successful if it has an active advisory committee made up of representatives of the leading agencies providing services to unmarried mothers and also some individuals who are deeply interested in this specific problem but who are not necessarily connected with a social agency.

A threefold service

In a few other cities somewhat different types of central services have been developed. For example, one agency, with a qualified case worker as the executive, offers a threefold service: Maternity-home care when desired and appropriate; care in a private family home when that seems best; or case-work service outside the home for any unmarried mother who decides she wants that help. The advantage of this plan is that one organization can itself provide whatever service a girl requires. Other agencies may continue to assist unmarried mothers who apply to them or may refer them to the specialized agency with the threefold service. That agency may refer young women to other agencies when advisable.

HOW PSYCHIATRY AND PSYCHOLOGY CAN HELP

Two resources that the case worker may call upon or may help an unmarried mother to utilize, if she needs either, are the services of a psychiatrist or a psychologist. As has been shown, the causes underlying the behavior that results in illegitimate pregnancy may be deep-seated within the individual. The behavior may be caused by an urge to solve old conflicts or by other emotional tensions. A psychiatrist, with his training in medicine and in the treatment of emotional disorders, can be exceedingly helpful to a disturbed unmarried mother. He can help her to understand her behavior and her attitudes and in many instances can free her sufficiently from anxiety so that she can go forward in planning more satisfactorily for herself and her baby. Or, through conferences with the case worker rather than the young woman, the psychiatrist may see diagnostic factors in the situation and make valuable suggestions for treatment. Unfortunately, however, psychiatric service is hard to obtain even when funds are available. There are relatively few psychiatrists in the whole country and only a small number of these have time or energy to expend on service to social agencies.

The service of a psychologist is utilized by many homes as a guide in helping an unmarried mother make her plans. Only a qualified psychologist—one who has done graduate work in clinical psychology and has had clinical experience under supervision—should be consulted. This specialist, with the aid of standardized tests and of other information supplied in advance of the test, including the young woman's developmental history, her interests, and her experience, can appraise her mental and emotional capacity and vocational aptitude.

The psychologist can also help in determining the mental capacity of the baby when adoption is being considered. Tests of babies are not so accurate as tests of older children and may have to be repeated at different periods in their development. Considered with other information about the baby, however, they provide a valuable safeguard in making decisions about placement.

After the tests have been given, the psychologist and case worker will discuss the results in relation to other factors and will interpret them in terms of the plans the mother is considering for her future and the future of the baby.

INCOMPLETE COORDINATION OF SERVICES

An attempt has been made in the previous pages to show the benefit that an unmarried mother and her baby can receive from a coordination of the services of a maternity home and of case work. At their best, these joint resources can be used by the mother to ease the difficulties of her readjustment and to give her baby a good start in life. But, because of different backgrounds, approaches, and skills, in the actual working out of local procedures, the two services do not always dovetail as they should. If this bulletin is to be helpful in these situations, it should suggest some of the causes of the failure of the services to complement each other effectively.

Unawareness of value

At present many homes fail to help the girl make the best use of the case-work services. Some homes think only of case work in relation to the girl who is troublesome or not adjusting well to the home, or if placement of the baby is desired. The resident who gives the impression of being fairly well adjusted, who is conforming to the routine of the home, and who seems to intend to keep her baby is considered not to be in need of case work. Many mothers, therefore, are deprived of the real help they seriously need—often because their need for it is so deep-seated that it is not easily recognized.

One probable reason for this lack of case-work service is an unawareness of its value on the part of superintendents and boards of directors. The superintendent who has had no training in social work and little contact with other social agencies may have had no chance to observe the help that an individual can receive from a case worker. She is, therefore, unable to interpret to the board and to the unmarried mother the basic value of case work to the mothers the home serves. Board members of maternity homes who have not served on the board of directors of other agencies may be unaware of how their own work would be strengthened by this service. State departments of public welfare and councils of social agencies that are mindful of this problem might suggest to other local social agencies the value of inviting a few progressive board members from each maternity home to serve on boards of other agencies.

Undefined duties

Closely allied to this lack of understanding of case work is the fact that in many communities no attempt has been made to define the duties of the superintendent of a maternity home and those of a professionally trained case worker. Each has an important place in service to unmarried mothers. The superintendent, even though she is trained in social work, has enough to do in giving leadership to the board, in taking part in other community activities, and in looking after the girls in the home without trying to do case work also. She should not be asked to give this service, particularly if her training has not been recent enough to include the newer concepts in case work, which is, of course, not static. If she has not been professionally trained in case work she should, obviously, no more attempt to fulfill the duties of a case worker than to take the place of a nurse or an obstetrician. In short, as an executive she should work with members of other professions rather than supplant them.

Guarding relations

Some homes question whether they can use case-work service from outside and still respect the confidences of an unmarried mother. They consider that their own staffs must provide all service that is given to her in order not to reveal information given to the home in confidence. This attitude is commendable in many ways. Maternity homes can feel assured, however, that they are not alone in their concern over protecting the information given by individuals who need assistance. It is the concern of all case-work agencies that the confidential relationship between case worker and client be guarded as carefully as that between priest and parishioner or doctor and patient. Much has been written in social-work literature on this subject.

The fact that social workers are a professional group should be recognized by those responsible for the work of maternity homes. If in a certain community a home has reason to believe that this professional attitude does not exist, or if evidence shows that confidential information has been revealed, the board of directors of the home should bring the matter to the attention of the agency or agencies responsible. It should be possible to work out procedures that will protect unmarried mothers in these situations.

Disappointment in services

Many times superintendents of maternity homes have found service from outside the home unsatisfactory. They have reported, with regret, that when they have asked for the assistance of another social agency, the service was disappointing. Some case workers have been content, these superintendents have reported, to interview an unmarried mother when she first enters the maternity home and then, because she is receiving good care and the birth of the child is not imminent, have not continued interviews with her for the purpose of planning. They have left the whole responsibility to the home until notified that the girl is ready to leave and that some plan must be made for her and the baby. It is no wonder under these circumstances that the superintendent believes she understands the girl better than does the case worker or that the board is not enthusiastic about case-work service.

Now and then a case worker shows a regrettable lack of reticence in an interview that may prejudice the unmarried mother and, through her, the home against case work in general. This case worker asks without reason the intimate questions that a prosecuting attorney might need to ask in preparing for court action. In doing so she forgets that a sensitive girl may not want to talk about some phase of her experience and will do so only if she must in order to answer questions for legal evidence.

The coin of disappointment has another side. Case workers have sometimes met with great difficulty in establishing relationships with residents of maternity homes. The case-work agency that refers a young woman to a home may not be allowed to continue service to her. Sometimes case workers are prevented from seeing mothers for 2 weeks at the time of their confinement—a period when they may especially need to see those close to them.

Some of the obstacles the workers encounter in homes are illustrated by a lack of privacy for interviews or refusal to permit a resident to leave the home for interviews. The reasons that superintendents frequently give for failure to make satisfactory arrangements are that case workers are not always thoughtful about timing their visits to the homes and that making special concessions for one mother would disrupt the routine of the home for the entire group.

A full measure of service

It is dangerous for any agency—maternity home or case-work agency—to have too possessive an attitude toward the persons who ask assistance and to be unwilling to share responsibility for treatment with another agency or individual qualified to supplement its work. It is dangerous, likewise, for individual staff members to become too possessive of those they serve. Staff members are most valuable when they have become aware of their own emotional needs; that is, when they have learned to understand why they think and act as they do day by day. Then, taking this knowledge into consideration in dealing with others, they are more likely to give objective, fruitful service. This is true regardless of whether they are staff members of an agency serving families or children or of a maternity home. Basically this is what everyone must strive to learn in order to become a real person. It is the key that case work tries to give—the ability to free one's own personality from its fetters.

This frank discussion of the fetters that bind some maternity-home and case-work agencies may help, it is hoped, to bring about uniform strength. It may start other discussions that will finally free this relationship of misunderstandings that now prevent a universally productive unity. Anything less robs unmarried mothers and their babies of a full measure of service.

New Interests Through Group Activities

The time an unmarried mother spends in a maternity home, however short, should be interesting and worthwhile. Making a recreational and educational program for her is not just to keep her busy in order to prevent boredom; nor is it primarily to get the work of the home accomplished. For some girls the mere act of living even for this short time in an atmosphere of serenity and orderliness has its values. If in addition they acquire the beginnings of new skills and new interests that they may develop in more detail when they leave the home, that is all to the good. Too great accomplishments cannot be expected from an educational program because of the difficulties of time and the situation. The young women are pregnant and therefore limited in their physical and social activities; some of the girls, emotionally disturbed, are not in a receptive frame of mind for new experiences; residents are entering and leaving the home constantly so that continuity of group activity is difficult, especially in small homes: the residents are different in age, interests, and background of home, school, work, and other experiences. Because of the constant change and the diversity, planning the daily activities of the group requires technical skill in program planning, imagination, ingenuity, and adaptability.

Through group activities a young woman may acquire an ability to get along well with other people, a better knowledge of herself and of what she wants to make of her life, some practical skills that make daily tasks more interesting, knowledge of where to go for information and assistance when she needs it, or new interests that she may wish to carry on in her precious leisure time when she is a wage earner or a busy housewife. No one girl will gain all of these tools for building her future, of course, and not all will need this type of service.

How the problems of each unmarried mother are worked out with her by the case worker has been discussed in the previous section, *The Value of Case-Work Service*. In addition to this individual counseling, the home can plan activities for the whole group that give both fun and knowledge. The case worker and the staff worker or volunteer responsible for group activities will, of course, work closely together in planning this group program. The case worker can contribute her technical knowledge of the basic difficulties that unmarried mothers face and her understanding of the individual residents of the home. The staff member who is responsible for program activities can contribute her skill in working with young people in a group.

Some suggestions for a program of activities are herewith offered that may be adapted to particular homes. The suggestions may be expanded or contracted to fit conditions in large or small homes, or changed to suit a home organized very differently from most homes. They do not pretend to be a complete program or a formula to follow because a program must be shaped by the type and resources of the home, the pattern of daily life there, and the choice of activities made by the girls living in the home at a given time.

What substance to give to the program and some ways to make it work are the topics of this section. Three activities are suggested: First, recreational and leisure-time activities; second, informal educational activities, including discussion groups, preparation for homemaking, and tutoring for incomplete studies; and, third, religious activities.

RECREATION AND LEISURE-TIME ACTIVITIES

Recreation touches many deep phases of life. Among them are the elemental desires for friendship, recognition, adventure, creative expression, and group acceptance. It offers values on which to draw for creating happy experiences for the unmarried mothers in a maternity home, individually and as a group. Recreation can start a young woman off toward expressing her interests in play so that what she gains will later help her to plan her leisure time wisely. She will then have wholesome outlets for her abilities and the energies that are characteristic of normal youth. The recreation planned for the residents should include a wide selection of activities—appropriate to the age and social development of all. It is a basic principle that each person decides whether she wants to participate and then makes her own choice of what is offered.

It is important that the staff realizes fully the value of recreation to unmarried mothers. As staff members know, many young women come to a maternity home partly as a result of unwise use of their leisure time. Some actually do not know how to play, their chief recreation having been found in "movies," dance halls, and unwholesome places of commercial amusement. Many of them are unaware of the resources within themselves that, if developed, would contribute greatly to their personal happiness. Knowing this should stimulate staff members to help the residents select and organize their leisure-time activities and recognize the possibilities of finding fun in simple ways.

Leadership from within the group should be encouraged—the kind of leadership that draws other girls into planning what the group wants to do. Many young women are not aware of their latent ability to work with others and to plan and organize until given opportunity to demonstrate what they can do. The timid, shy girl may have her whole attitude toward herself and society changed to her advantage through gaining the sincere approval of the group she lives with for this brief period of her life. The domineering, aggressive girl may be helped to find an acceptable place in the group and to gain the approval of her companions.

Qualified leadership

It is desirable for the recreation program in the home to be planned and developed by workers trained and experienced in the field of group work and recreation. Few homes have a group worker on the staff or can afford to employ one for full time or even for part time. Instead, these homes must call on other agencies in the community for assistance in building up recreational activities. The council of social agencies may be able to make the arrangements. Local private and public agencies in the field can perhaps give their services, either in an advisory capacity or by lending leaders from their staffs for short periods of time for special activities, or both. Some of these agencies are the public schools, municipal recreation departments, the YWCA, social settlements, community centers, and the Girl Scouts. All have staff members qualified to act as consultants as well as workers who might be sent to the home for special projects.

The home should assign the staff member or volunteer who has the greatest aptitude for this kind of work to act as the liaison between the home and the advisory agency. This staff member or volunteer should carry out the advice of the consultant and arrange for the leader lent by an agency to develop some definite part of the program. The staff member should help the leader in advance of the visit to understand the work of the home and the sensitivities of unmarried mothers. She should also tell the residents about the leader in advance and then help them get acquainted easily so that the leader and group can immediately work closely together.

Indoor activities

In planning recreation it is well to include quiet and active types for both indoor and outdoor programs. The advice of the medical staff will, of course, govern the extent to which the girls take part in physical activities. The daily program of the home should be arranged so that free time is possible for each resident and time is allotted to planned group activities. Space, equipment, and supplies are necessary for recreational activities. Whenever possible a recreation room, separate from the regular lounge or living room, should be arranged for in which some girls can do handicraft, rehearse informal dramatics and music, and plan activities, such as parties, without disturbing other girls. This room should be made comfortable and attractive by use of bright colored draperies, good pictures, rugs, lamps, tables and easy chairs, a radio or phonograph, a piano, and cabinets for storing games and equipment when not in use.

Table games.—There is no better way to develop friendly, understanding, and happy relationships between the girls than through wholesome intragroup activity. To make this possible, indoor activities can be developed, for example, table tennis, ping pong, Chinese checkers, backgammon, and card games.

Music.—Music offers many possibilities for individuals and groups. Listening to music may be more than an enjoyment in itself; it may stimulate a girl's interest in developing latent musical talent or in continuing interrupted study. Radio broadcasts—the time and stations carefully followed by one person in order to get the good programs—and phonograph records offer opportunity to hear the greatest artists and also to keep in touch with currently popular dance music. Informal group singing can be fun if a good leader is available within the home or from some community agency. Choral and part singing might even grow, with good leadership, into an informal glee club that could work toward songs for special days of celebration in the home.

Music can give intangible satisfactions. The superintendent of one small home, for example, has found this to be true. She has a phonograph in her own centrally located room. Often when the residents seem unusually restless or tense or a current of discord goes through the house, the superintendent starts playing a record. The music flows out through the halls and rooms of the home and after a while the restlessness or tension subsides. The three records she most frequently plays in this way are The Lord's Prayer, sung by John Charles Thomas, and Panis Angelicus and Ave Maria, sung by Beniamino Gigli. Often they are asked for just after the residents have gone to bed.

The screen.—Sixteen-millimeter motion pictures that are of interest to young people can be a welcome diversion during leisure time if they are well selected. Should the home have no portable projection machine and be unable to buy one, a board member might be able to obtain one on loan for special occasions.

These home-shown pictures are of particular value if the maternity home is far from the theaters in the community or when bad weather keeps the residents inside. Visual slides and stereopticon views as well as films on travel, vocations, and hundreds of other topics can be obtained at small cost through most State departments of education and other sources. The public-relations secretary of the local council of social agencies may be consulted about obtaining films suitable for young people. Current "shorts" that are shown at regular theaters can be arranged for through local motion-picture theaters or distributing offices at reasonable cost. If showings are planned well in advance the residents will have a chance to assist in selecting the films and arranging the programs.

Good motion-picture films made by amateurs on trips to other countries or to interesting parts of this country can give a great deal of pleasure. Local camera clubs will give suggestions about obtaining these films for a showing. Board or staff members may have friends who are camera enthusiasts and have taken motion pictures that might be shown or who at least might suggest ways to obtain films. Some amateur colored motion pictures of peoples of other lands not only are beautiful to see but stimulate reading about these far-away countries.

Arts and crafts.—Individuals and groups may enjoy different types of arts and crafts and get from them an idea of their manual ability. Young women may choose their own interests and hobbies after they have had chances to experiment with different kinds of handwork. Some of these activities are block printing of different kinds, drawing, sketching, water-color and finger painting, weaving, carving, clay modeling, sewing, making collections of certain items, and making decorative posters.

An interest in a handcraft or in collecting that grows into a hobby may become more than a pastime; it may be an absorbing pleasure for years. Such a hobby may open new avenues of information and lead to new, congenial acquaintanceships.

Community projects.—Taking part in community projects gives the residents a chance to make a contribution to neighborhood and national life. The council of social agencies may suggest community projects functioning in the city that are suitable for residents of a home.

Reading.—An interest in reading can be one of the most absorbing and rewarding habits a young person can acquire. For this reason most homes try to make good, up-to-date reading matter easily accessible to their residents. Books that are near at hand and can be picked up in a moment of free time are more of a temptation than those neatly tucked away on shelves in a special room.

An adequate and suitable supply of books, magazines, and daily newspapers is essential. The books may range from attractively illustrated though inexpensive children's books, so that the mothers may learn what books are being published for children, to those on such subjects as fast-moving current history. There should be good novels, biographies of persons of interest to young people, and books on current events. Books on the care of babies, on homemaking, jobs and job getting, good grooming and choice of clothes, books on travel—with pictures—and on different hobbies and the materials used in hobbies will be welcome. The library should have a standard encyclopedia and an up-to-date unabridged dictionary.

Magazines should be chosen for their easy readability. For example, the women's magazines have a convenient combination of story and practical suggestions about clothes, personal appearance, and other things that interest girls. Magazines on gardening, sports, or good health will be apt to have many readers in the home. A picture magazine will be welcome for swift reviews of what is happening in the world. At least one daily newspaper will of course be part of the "library" service, with enough copies for all to read.

If used books and magazines are offered to the home by board members or by groups interested in the home, they should be accepted only if they are appropriate for young people, of current interest, and in good condition. It is best to keep the book supply growing by additions of new volumes bought from time to time by funds appropriated by the board for this purpose. If gifts are depended on entirely, it is well to have ready to give to prospective donors a list of books and magazines that are especially wanted. That will give them an idea of the type of reading matter the residents like.

The local public library will be of great help in building up a collection of books for a home. Advice as to what books to buy, lists of reading on specific subjects for individual readers, and the loan of a collection of books suitable for the residents for a given time are some of the services the home may obtain from a well-equipped public library. The superintendent will find it exceedingly profitable to know the librarians and to have them know about the educational and recreational activities of the home. They may make excellent suggestions about ways to help young people form good reading habits that will always stand them in good stead.

Besides the inside-the-home service, the public library can give assistance at the library. Many of the unmarried mothers knew their home-town library before they came to the home and need only to be told where the nearest library is to start "getting books out" again. The girls who never had the library habit might, with encouragement, go there to see what this treasury of books holds for them. They might want to see the building itself, how the library operates, and how the books are displayed to catch the eye of a reader; to browse among the magazines; to see an exhibit of pictures. of handicrafts, of ancient pewter, perhaps; and to hear of such services as readers' advisers who will answer questions, make out lists on special subjects, or help readers find the information that they want. This introduction may lead to use of libraries in later days in other places.

Dramatics.—Dramatics may be a particularly helpful activity for girls in a maternity home. Through this outlet they may express themselves without reticence because in "play acting" they can afford to be ficticious persons. A skilled dramatic leader would be helpful if she understood these particular young women.

The dramatization of special events and holidays is always of interest to young people. With the help of staff members the residents can present in an informal way short skits, plays, and simple pageants. These can be given on Saturday nights or special occasions. This is not only a means of good fun, but is an excellent way to exercise imagination and to develop confidence, self-expression, and ingenuity. Some of the girls will be more interested in preparing the costumes and settings than in acting.

Informal indoor fun.—Simple informal types of seasonal group recreation that call for little expense, time, and energy are candy pulls, popcorn parties, festival celebrations such as Halloween, and the like. When certain materials are scarce, ingenuity is needed to plan such gatherings. In one home, before bedtime each winter night the residents gather in the large, comfortable kitchen for a "nightcap" of coffee or chocolate, which they prepare. A visitor to the home on one occasion was invited to join them. The girls decided that they would eat as usual in the kitchen rather than make the occasion formal by using the living room. They wished the visitor to feel that she was part of the group. When the guest arrived she found that the residents had whipped up a coffee cake as a surprise to her. Over their cake and beverage they sat around the table and chatted about various subjects of interest to the girls. In this type of informal gathering, opportunity frequently arises to talk about matters that relate to the life of the group as a whole that would be difficult to discuss under more formal conditions.

Out-of-doors recreation

In the garden.—Because pregnant women need fresh air and plenty of sunshine, out-of-doors recreation can be encouraged. The yard and porch space of the home should be equipped with plenty of swings or gliders, chairs and benches, to accommodate the residents. Tables are convenient to use while doing handwork of any kind or playing table games. Eating out-of-doors is pleasant in the right season. An outdoor oven for cooking picnic suppers makes an inexpensive and enjoyable way of changing the routine of the evening meal.

Some will enjoy growing flowers and tending small plots of vegetables, either as a familiar or a new experience. This gardening will mean more to the gardener if it is not compulsory work and she can choose her own planting and use the products as she wishes. The home may have its own plot of ground that the residents can use or may obtain a plot suitable for their use through a community gardening project.

One outdoor game that can be adapted to the physical conditions of the girls is croquet. Other games, such as shuffle board and darts, may be adapted also but should be planned for only in consultation with the staff physician.

Recreation away from the home.—Some girls do not want to feel cut off from outside activities. They want to go out and get a feeling of belonging to the community rather than avoiding contact with it. They may want to go to concerts, museums, art galleries, department stores, motion pictures, or to the theater. One girl may want to go alone if the trip is one in which she only is interested but most of the girls will probably want to go with other residents or with relatives or friends. Freedom to go without a staff member if they know how to get around in town will be appreciated by the girls. In turn, they will observe the ordinary courtesy of any daughter to her parents— to let the home know where she is going and when she expects to be back.

Young women who have never known the quiet pleasure that can be found in group picnics and walks may find it during this stay in a maternity home. Walks in botanical gardens, or the wooded parts of city parks with someone who knows about trees, flowers, plants, and birds may open new avenues of interest and lead to more ambitious walking later on. After learning that walking can be fun, two or three girls may go out together to walk in woods or parks near the home or conveniently reached by trolley or bus—wherever they will not feel conspicuous as a group. Most cities have organized groups for nature study and outings that can supply information on walks of different lengths and of different interests.

INFORMAL EDUCATIONAL ACTIVITIES

Just as the recreational activities are planned to make the residents' brief stay in the home interesting, so the informal educational activities are planned with the same aim. If, in addition, a girl acquires the beginnings of new skills, more useful information, perhaps some "credits," plus a desire to go deeper into these new interests, that is a gain she may later value greatly. Some subjects that will be of interest are suggested here, along with some informal ways of presenting the topics to the group. A skillful leader, in planning the activities of the residents, will encourage them to reveal their interests and will then use these interests in planning an appealing program. How can educational material be offered in an informal and enjoyable way?

Discussion groups

In a series of informal discussions under leadership, almost any of the subjects of interest and value to the residents may be presented— if qualified leaders can be found. One leader may conduct a whole series or several leaders may take up different parts of a subject.

The choice of a discussion leader is most important, because this work, seeming so simple, in reality takes great skill and much experience. Possibly some member of the staff has this skill and experience, for instance, the physician, the nurse, the case worker, or the one who supervises the program of activities. All may be qualified as far as subject matter is concerned but none may be a good discussion leader. Leaders from outside can be found in adult-education groups, in private and public agencies serving youth, public-health agencies, child-study associations, child-guidance agencies, family and children's agencies, libraries, on faculties of local high schools, colleges, or universities.

Before appointing a leader the superintendent should be sure that the leader understands the difficulties of the residents and is sympathetic with them. Otherwise, the leader may unintentionally defeat the purpose of the discussions by arousing resentment instead of an interested desire to talk things over. The residents will be more interested in the series if they hear in advance about the background and accomplishment of each leader.

To keep the atmosphere of the meetings informal and as different as possible from that of a schoolroom is essential. Ways of conducting the meetings should vary from time to time. At some, discussion-provoking motion pictures or still pictures might be shown, at others, exhibits of collections made as a hobby or of handicrafts might be on display to illustrate some point under discussion. Short stories, articles, or books could be used as a basis for conversation. The leader could start by reading aloud a story or a passage from a book, perhaps dealing with family life, and follow the reading with a summary of the book. The leader will weave in suggestions about sources of further information.

The group that chooses a series could meet as often as twice a week at times when the mothers will not be too tired and when the period is guarded from interruption. The number of times the group meets, the content of the discussion and the way the leader organizes her material will be determined by the number of residents who will be present for 6 weeks or 2 months. The informal talks may have a value apart from their subject matter. They may increase the girls' self-confidence in expressing their opinions and in contributing points to a general conversation in an effective way.

As an example of what is meant by a discussion series, a brief outline is given below of practical talks about the care and guidance of children. This subject will be of immediate interest to many of the unmarried mothers—to those who plan to keep their babies, those who expect to marry later, and those who may do domestic work. The mothers who are giving up their babies should not be included in this group unless they specifically choose to join. The outline, divided into six topics, might cover a period of 6 weeks, with two meetings on each topic. Much of the time may be taken up in talking about actual happenings brought up by members of the group to illustrate points discussed.

ESSENTIALS OF CHILD CARE AND GUIDANCE

What all of us should know about children in order to be responsive to their needs:

I. *How to care for children physically.*
   How they grow, how to feed them, how to protect their health, how the physical well-being of children depends upon the love and affection that underlie their care.

II. *How to give opportunities for the development of their minds.*
   What play means to children's development; how their surroundings help or hinder the expansion of their interests and efforts; the

54

importance of adults' comradeship with children through reading, conversation, and trips for exploring their environment.

III. *How to understand the feelings of children and to help them to control and direct their strong desires.*

Appreciation of their desire to do things "on their own," of their need for independence and for experimentation (examples: dressing and eating), and of their desire to have others enjoy and respond to them.

IV. *How to guide the habits of children.*

How children learn. (Laws of learning as applied to eating, sleeping, eliminating, and so forth.)

How the habits of adults affect children. (Example: an adult who is consistent in his treatment of a child gives him a feeling of security and safety; an adult who is well adjusted creates an atmosphere of harmony and order that contributes to a child's acceptance of guidance.)

V. *How to understand the stages of growth of children and the peculiar problems of each stage.*

Infancy: The protection from fear, as well as from disease.

The toddler stage: Why children must learn through their senses.

The period of resistance to authority: How to handle displays of temper.

The period of questioning: Answers to questions children ask about their bodies are as important as responses to other inquiries.

The period of imagination: Why imagination is important; how to deal with it.

VI. *How to create a happy home.*

The kind of house a child lives in, the kind of clothes he wears, or the toys he has are of far less importance than his feeling of being wanted and loved. (Example: a child can stand a terrifying experience if he is with his mother and feels sure of her affection for him.)

The quality of the relations between the adults with whom a child lives forms the basis for his learning the values of family life. If there are several children in a home, it is important that the adults recognize each child as an individual with special needs.

Subjects for discussion

The content of an educational program for the unmarried mothers in a home is essentially the same as for any group of girls of the same age range. Because of pregnancy, some girls will have more than ordinary interest in certain subjects; others may show less interest in what appealed to them before. In general, young women are concerned about how to earn a living, their relationship to others, freedom of action, and assuming the responsibilities of adulthood. Questions about these subjects will always be talked about, perhaps in very simple terms, whenever girls get together in a group. A few topics under these broad subjects are herewith given that might be discussed in groups.[1]

Many of the unmarried mothers in a home will have been employed in jobs with a future in which they were competent and happy. Others who have been in dead-end jobs because, perhaps, they lacked skills may have disliked their work. Still others have never worked for a living. Some girls, particularly those from small towns and farms, may have had no opportunity to learn of the many occupations open to women and of the contributions that women have made to business and industry. Well-planned discussions on these points will be of help to all young women but particularly to those who would like a change of employment or who are planning employment for the first time.

Another pertinent subject, but one that needs skillful handling, centers around a girl's relationship to other people. Each leader might present the subject matter in a different way, according to her background and occupation. The case worker versed in leading discussions might explore this topic with the unmarried mothers and in so doing give them some insight into the reasons back of human behavior. Another leader might develop the subject from the standpoint of family relationships—what makes a family and why some families get along well together and others do not. Or the leader might think in terms of the development of personality—what qualities persons like in others and how individuals can learn to lead more satisfying lives.

Most girls are interested in personal attractiveness. It might be wise to have talks centered on this topic as part of a series on health aimed to give the mothers more understanding of physiology and of the importance of rest, food, and physical activity. This leads naturally into the subject of good grooming—care of the body and clothing suitable to a girl and her activities, planned on a knowledge of the quality of fabrics, of color, and of becoming lines.

Spontaneous discussions

That "leaders" and "series" have been suggested in the preceding paragraphs does not mean that no significant discussions will take place without planning or thought in advance. Many come about under any circumstances in any group living under one roof or seeing one another

---

[1] Subject matter for informal recreational and educational programs that can be adapted to the use of maternity homes has been developed by such organizations as the Young Women's Christian Association, 600 Lexington Ave., New York 22, N. Y., and the Association for Family Living, 209 So. State St., Chicago 4, Ill.

often. Spontaneous discussions may begin in a flash during a meal, during a game of cards while one player is dealing, or while a number of residents are walking home from the "movies." When a staff member happens to be one of the group that starts such a discussion, she may see a chance to throw in, by a casual remark, some information that is needed or to focus more attention on a vital point that the talk is skirting. Or she may just keep the discussion lively by being an intent listener.

Some superintendents, who appreciate the value of this spontaneous "hashing over" of topics that concern young people, make opportunities for them consciously but not obviously. The superintendents bring about comfortable and easy times of sitting around a friendly open fire in winter or in a cool corner of the garden on a summer afternoon. Conversation develops naturally, perhaps out of something a girl has done that day or from news in a letter from home or in a newspaper item. Some shy girls may be brought into the conversation by a question from an alert adult who is just one of the talkers, decidedly in the background. As unobtrusively and naturally as possible the staff member seeks to maintain the continuity of the conversation as long as active interest is evident. The value of this type of spontaneous discussion is that the unmarried mothers, relaxed and unselfconscious in expressing themselves, may make points of depth and significance that they would not bring up in more organized conversations.

Preparation for homemaking

The work that residents do in a home offers a good opportunity to give them both skills and a sense of achievement. Persons supervising their work should be understanding, practical, and able to teach efficient practices in home management. They should also know that the duties of the mothers should be adjusted to their physical condition on advice of the physician. Good supervisors will find ways to give pride in a job well done. Homemaking can be a joy or a drudgery; the girl's attitude toward it and her command of efficient methods of work largely determine the outcome for her.

It is important that food served in the home be interesting and appetizing as well as nutritious. (*See* p. 68 for the foods expectant mothers need daily and menus including them.) Residents can be taught the planning of nutritious meals, and the selecting, buying, preparing, and serving of food. Some homes have found one of the most popular activities to be the combined cooking and nutrition classes taught by carefully chosen home economists. One small home has arranged with the local superintendent of schools for classes taught by a home-economics teacher in the homemaking classrooms of a nearby school. The classes are held during the early evening when the building is not otherwise in use. In this way the residents are given professional instruction and the advantages of school equipment. At the same time, the routine of the home's kitchen is not slowed by teaching.

Knowing how to mend, launder, iron, remove spots, or press clothing is a decided help to good grooming that will be useful wherever a young woman may be. Young women who are handy with a needle or who can be taught to be will find this skill an asset toward having a greater variety of blouses, simple dresses, and clothes accessories. Learning to use patterns and to remodel dresses are invaluable aids to being well dressed, especially if the clothing budget is slim. Discussion of money-management problems as related to these various aspects of homemaking can be most helpful when conducted by a skilled leader.

Taking pride in a job well done has a close connection with wage earning as well as with homemaking. Good work habits are an invaluable asset in employment. The residents can be encouraged to take full responsibility for assignments after they understand their instructions and to tie up all the loose ends of a long job before they consider it finished. This is decidedly a part of group activity because recognition on the part of the staff or of other residents of a job well done gives a girl a sense of achievement that can make work a satisfaction.

Tutoring for incomplete studies

Closely bound up with employment is the problem of uncompleted education. The girl whose schooling has been interrupted by pregnancy may decide after talks with the case worker that it is wise for her to complete some part of her education. In some cases, it may be wise for the case worker to arrange for consultation with a vocational advisor or a psychologist. A girl may want to study while in the home in order to use this time to advantage. It may be wise for other girls who have already dropped out of school to try to pick up the loose threads while in the home as a test of whether further school work is practicable. A qualified psychologist can be helpful to the case worker in all these decisions.

Many maternity homes have arranged with the local school authorities for the services of a teacher. One home reports that for a period of years its educational program has worked well to the great satisfaction and enjoyment of the residents. A teacher with wide experience as a substitute in the public schools was assigned to the home by the board of education and was given the school authorities' enthusiastic support. The girls assist with the work of the home from breakfast until 11 a. m. They are then free for the activities they have chosen. Those who are to do classroom work go to the room equipped for school purposes. Classes are informal and as little like the disciplined, ordinary classroom as possible, because some of the girls have resisted school previously, considering it humdrum and boring. Classes last 30 minutes and are so arranged that girls who need rest can have it. The classes are small and are organized so that the teacher can divide her attention between groups that are busy studying while others are carrying on class discussions. One of the important features is that the time is carefully guarded against interruption. Because the classes are small, they can be planned to meet the requirements and interests of each resident. The superintendent of schools, whose interest originally made the plan possible, has arranged that the girls get credit for completed work, the certificates being issued from the nearest elementary or high school without the name of the maternity home appearing. Credits so earned are accepted anywhere in the State.

These classes have meant so much to some girls that they have kept in touch with the instructor after leaving the home when their jobs prevented them from taking courses at night schools. They have come back to get assignments, submit written material, and discuss various "problems" with the teacher.

RELIGIOUS ACTIVITIES

The social worker undoubtedly will discover in her work with unmarried mothers what part religion has played in each one's life, its present meaning to her, and how she can use it. The girls who come to a maternity home have their inner conflicts and undefined longings just as most young people have, but theirs are intensified by this crisis in their lives. Some of the young women who have already had satisfying religious experience can get comfort from their religion and should be given every opportunity and encouragement in this. Others have never had any religious influence or instruction. Still others feel bitterness toward religion because of unhappy experiences they have had in their own homes with "religious" parents who showed a rigidly moralistic attitude toward their children's normal desire for fun. Still others are indifferent to religion, thinking of it as merely formal church services with a tedious sermon without any meaning for them.

Spiritual values have a place in everyone's life. Some build and express them in one way; others in another. Some do this best within the frame of formal religion through a lifetime of church devotion. Others have broken their church connections by nonconformance to the outward expression of the tenets of their churches. They feel that they can still maintain spiritual values without formal religious observance. These individuals often renew their connections with a church when they are in serious trouble. They may find comfort and strength through consultation with a pastor of a church or through attendance at religious services.

Many maternity homes conduct their own religious services. The home functioning under church auspices often has a regularly assigned chaplain. He arranges for all the services that are appropriate. This plan has great advantages in that the clergyman learns to know the residents and their difficulties and can plan continuity of religious instruction. Other homes rely for their religious services on pastors of different churches or on lay religious groups. Each pastor or group may come to the home on only one occasion or may take part in a series of meetings.

The services that are held in the home should be carefully planned. They should have dignity and beauty and, most surely, warmth and meaning for these particular girls. These qualities are more likely to be attained if whatever talks are given aim at a way of life that will be rich in worth-while experience and satisfying to the one who lives it and if nothing is said that might build up in any unmarried mother feelings of guilt that might make her less capable of dealing with the future. Everything said should help her to think hopefully of the years ahead.

The qualifications of the clergymen who are invited to conduct services should be considered with exceeding care. They should include friendly understanding of young people and a knowledge of how to talk to those who are out of step with accepted standards of conduct. Visits from pastors or church groups that have not been carefully planned in relation to the residents' interests may alienate unmarried mothers rather than help them. The principle to remember is to invite only the most suitable persons—those able to create a spiritual atmosphere and to adapt programs to a special group of young people.

In planning the religious services the staff member responsible may want to enlist the help of the residents. Some of them may enjoy arranging the setting, the flowers, chairs, books, and so forth, or even taking more responsibility. They will certainly enjoy planning programs for special occasions such as Thanksgiving, Christmas, and Easter when simple pageants or carol services may be given.

Even if the home has its own religious services, some residents may wish to attend regular church services in the community. Those who feel comfortable in doing so should be encouraged to go. Many girls from small places may get inspiration from services unfamiliar to them, for instance, the richness of services in some large city churches. Furthermore, the girl who has not been a regular church attendant may be more likely to continue attendance in church if she forms the habit under stimulating circumstances while she is in the home. She may find a congenial companion who wishes to go to church for the same reasons as hers, and so begin in this natural way a whole new religious experience.

Health and Medical Services[1]

Preceding sections of the bulletin have discussed services that should be available to an unmarried mother because of the complexities that face her during pregnancy and the period of social adjustment after the birth of her child. This section outlines the health and medical care that she should receive. That this care should be of the same high standard that a married mother should receive would seem to be too obvious to mention. Unfortunately, however, most women who are illegitimately pregnant receive unsatisfactory maternity care as compared with pregnant married women. The chief reason for this difference is the lateness in pregnancy when unmarried mothers usually come under medical supervision—often as late as the sixth month. The social stigma attached to pregnancy without marriage is likely to cause a girl to take the risk of concealing her condition as long as possible. It is the responsibility of individuals or agencies who may come into contact with pregnant unmarried girls to see that they get under a physician's care promptly. If an unmarried mother applies to a maternity home early in pregnancy and plans to enter later, the home will, of course, make sure that she has good medical care in the interim.

---

[1] Prepared by Barbara A. Hewell, M. D., of the Division of Research in Child Development, in cooperation with John L. Parks, M. D., the Children's Bureau's consultant in obstetrics, and Marjorie M. Heseltine, consultant in nutrition of the Division of Health Services.

Another reason for some of the unsatisfactory maternity care that unmarried mothers receive, and one especially pertinent to this discussion, is that many maternity homes—small institutions, modestly financed—cannot provide the quality of medical service that the facilities and qualified personnel of large, well-equipped hospitals and clinics can offer. Conditions do vary greatly as to the availability of community or hospital prenatal clinics and services but when they are available it is wise for small maternity homes to consider using these clinics and services for prenatal, delivery, and postpartum care rather than continuing or setting up a separate service.

Good maternity care requires expensive equipment, aseptic techniques, safe anesthesia, provision for emergency treatment—such as transfusions—and expert medical and nursing services. It is often impossible for small maternity homes to furnish them. Some of these homes may be able to provide adequate prenatal supervision and safe delivery care for patients without complications. The home should, however, arrange with hospitals for the observation and delivery of patients with complications or whose delivery may be difficult. For large maternity homes in which many deliveries occur, the expense of the complete service may be justified.

The medical and nursing services offered by the maternity home will vary according to whether the complete care is given in the home by staff physicians and nurses or whether community clinics and hospitals are used for prenatal, delivery, and postpartum care. In the latter case, the staff physicians and nurses will give general supervision and will coordinate the home, clinic, and hospital services. The emphasis in the health and medical program will be on the hygiene of pregnancy, the prevention of complications, prompt referral to clinic or hospital of all abnormalities, the care of infants, and late postpartum supervision. When the complete service is given in the home, prenatal examinations, delivery care, and immediate postpartum care of mother and care of the infant will also be an important part of the medical program.

The health of the mother during pregnancy affects the course of labor and delivery, the condition of the infant, and later the health of the mother. Adequate food during pregnancy is essential. The living conditions in the maternity home, the social adjustments of the residents, the program of activities described in the section *New Interests Through Group Activities*, have an important bearing on the physical and mental health of the unmarried mothers in the home.

In this section suggestions are given in outline form under the following eight headings: (1) Medical supervision, including advisory and attending staff; (2) nursing service; (3) prenatal care, including medical services, supervision of diet, and hygiene of pregnancy; (4) delivery service; (5) postpartum care; (6) care of infants; (7) facilities for medical and nursing care of mothers; and (8) facilities for medical and nursing care of infants.

Only the essential points in the provision of health supervision and medical services are included but references are given for more detailed information. The extent of facilities and services needed will, of course, vary with the type and size of the maternity home.

MEDICAL SUPERVISION

The medical advisory committee of the home should include specialists in obstetrics, pediatrics, nursing, and social work. The committee should have general responsibilities, such as organizing the medical program; establishing policies, procedures, and standards of care; arranging cooperative relationships with hospitals or other medical agencies; selecting staff physicians and determining their responsibilities; approving nursing staff appointments; and providing clinical consultation upon the request of the staff.

Consultation of the superintendent of the home and the medical advisory committee with the director of the maternal and child-health division of the State health department and the director of the child-welfare division of the State welfare department will be helpful in planning the health and medical policies, procedures, and program. For the States that license and supervise maternity homes, one or both of these departments—health and welfare—have the responsibility of licensing and supervision and are therefore interested in standards of care.

The staff of attending physicians should have direct responsibility for the health supervision and medical care of the women residents in the home and their infants, according to the policies, procedures, and standards established by the medical advisory committee. The staff should include physicians who have had training and experience in obstetrics, pediatrics, and general medicine.

A. Responsibilities of the staff obstetrician

1. To supervise all health aspects of the program for care of women in the home.

2. To provide prenatal, delivery, and postpartum care unless these services are provided at clinics and hospitals.

3. To coordinate the program in the home with recommendations of physicians in the prenatal clinic so that the women will be able to follow out the instructions given in the clinic.

676781°—46—5

4. To give any prenatal care that may be necessary in addition to that given in the prenatal clinic and to arrange for care in appropriate clinics or hospitals for remedial work, illnesses, or complications of pregnancy.

5. To be on call in case of obstetric emergency.

6. To be responsible for isolation of any woman with an infectious condition and for her transfer to a hospital when indicated.

7. To request consultation when indicated.

8. To keep a record of the obstetric and medical history of every woman admitted to the home.

9. To consult with the case worker regarding problems that call for joint decision or action (for example, mental hygiene, work. recreation, or medical follow-up after discharge).

B. **Responsibilities of the staff pediatrician**

1. To supervise all health aspects of the care of infants in the home.

2. To give regular medical supervision to all infants in the home, unless this has been arranged for in a child-health conference or well-baby clinic. Such supervision will include initial and periodic medical examination, direction of feeding, and daily care.

3. To give medical care to sick infants or those presenting any abnormality or to provide for their care at appropriate clinics or hospitals.

4. To be on call for pediatric emergency.

5. To be responsible for the isolation of any infants having or suspected of having infectious conditions.

6. To request consultation when indicated.

7. To keep a record of the health history of each infant.

8. To consult with the case worker regarding problems that call for joint decision or action (discontinuance of breast feeding. suitability of the baby for placement, or medical follow-up after discharge).

C. *The staff physician* who is responsible for general medical care should be on call in case of illness not directly associated with pregnancy, as, for example, for upper respiratory infections and communicable diseases. He should be responsible for consultation service to the staff regarding diagnosis and treatment of medical conditions.

NURSING SERVICE

The administration of the nursing service should be under the direction of a registered graduate nurse who has had postgraduate preparation and experience in obstetric nursing and in the care of infants.

A.   Responsibilities of the supervisor

1. In cooperation with the medical staff, to develop nursing procedures, techniques, routines, and standing orders to be used in the care of maternity patients and their infants.

2. To supervise and instruct the nursing staff in the policies and procedures to be followed in the care of mothers and infants.

3. To maintain equipment and supplies essential to good nursing care of mothers and infants.

4. To see that adequate nursing service is provided on a 24-hour basis for all mothers and infants. This service should be sufficient to provide assistance to physicians for necessary examinations and treatment.

5. To direct the supervision of all practical nurses, nurses' aides, and auxiliary workers.

6. To report promptly to the physician any evidence of abnormality in mother or infant.

7. To see that complete and accurate nursing records and reports are kept for all mothers and infants.

8. To supervise the preparation of milk mixtures and other feedings for infants.

9. To plan for instruction of the mothers in prenatal and postpartum care and the care of their infants.

10. To cooperate with the case worker in providing for follow-up nursing care of mothers and infants after their discharge.

B.   Size of nursing staff

The nursing staff should be sufficient in number to have one member on duty at all times. This should be a graduate nurse. If there is only one graduate nurse, she should live in the home and be on call by the attendant in case of emergency. Additional nursing service should be provided for emergency situations such as an unusual number of deliveries or the serious illness of mothers or infants.

Because the number of nurses needed will vary with the patient load, it is impossible to give a ratio of nurses to patients that would apply to the situation in different maternity homes. The following ratios are desirable: for the delivery room, 2 nurses per patient in labor; for postpartum care, 1 nurse to 5 patients by day and to 10 by night; for infants, 1 nurse to 8 full-term newborn infants and 1 nurse to 4 premature infants by day and night.

PRENATAL CARE

Prenatal care in the home or in a clinic should include:

A. **Medical services**

   (*See* Children's Bureau publication 153, *Standards of Prenatal Care; an outline for the use of physicians.*)

   1. A complete medical and obstetric history upon admission to the home.

   2. A complete physical examination, including external abdominal and internal pelvic examination and pelvic measurements. This should be done by the staff or clinic physician when the unmarried mother first comes under the medical supervision of the home. This is usually done early in pregnancy but even though a record is obtained from the woman's physician, a complete check should be made by the physician who will deliver the patient.

      Every possible effort should be made by the home to have the unmarried mothers receive adequate early prenatal care before entry to the home.

   3. The admission examination should include blood pressure determination, weight, urinalysis, a blood test for syphilis, urethral and cervical smear and culture for gonorrheal infection, determination of hemoglobin, red and white blood cell counts, and any other special studies that may be indicated.

      A short period of isolation of new admissions should be observed until venereal infection has been ruled out. Although negative reports of Wassermann test and vaginal smear have been received prior to admission, it will be safer to recheck.

66

Patients with syphilis and gonorrhea can usually be rendered noninfectious in a few weeks by modern methods of treatment. If such treatment can be given, there is no reason why women with these conditions cannot be cared for in the home.

4. Dental examination followed by treatment indicated.

5. Regular medical supervision. The physician should examine the patient at least once a month in the first 6 months of pregnancy, twice a month in seventh and eighth months, weekly during the ninth month, and more often if indicated. Blood pressure, weight, height of fundus, fetal heart tones, fetal position, and urine should be checked at each of these examinations.

At these regular visits the physician will discuss with the mother such topics as diet, exercise, hygiene measures, or any special problems and make specific suggestions to be followed out.

The weekly menus of the home should be reviewed by the physician. The maternity home should allow sufficient funds in the budget to provide food that is adequate in quality and quantity.

6. Treatment of abnormal conditions. Any complications of pregnancy or other illness should be promptly recognized and the appropriate treatment given. Treatment for syphilis should be begun early in pregnancy and continue through pregnancy and after childbirth.

7. Adequate clinical records, both medical and nursing. If prenatal care is given at an outside clinic, significant findings and instructions should be available from the clinic for the maternity-home record form.

B. Supervision of diet

One of the most important considerations in the health program of the home is the provision of adequate food for the women during pregnancy, as proper nutrition is essential for the health of both mother and infant. Because unmarried mothers tend to come under medical supervision late in pregnancy, many of them will have had inadequate diets during the early months of pregnancy. Their nutrition will need special consideration. The physician will outline the essentials of the diet for the home and will prescribe modifications or special diets as indicated for individual expectant mothers.

The larger homes may be able to employ a full or part-time dietitian to supervise this program. In the smaller homes the staff member responsible for planning the diet should be able to obtain information and suggestions from home economists or nutritionists from departments of health or welfare, or other qualified agencies in the local community. In most States consultation service may be obtained from the nutritionist on the staff of the State health department.

1. The food needs of the pregnant woman and her baby will be met if enough food is provided so that each expectant mother receives every day:

> Milk: One quart.
> Vegetables and fruits: Five or six servings (not necessarily different vegetables).
>> Potato.
>> A green leafy or deep yellow vegetable.
>> A raw vegetable or fruit.
>> A fruit or vegetable rich in vitamin C.
>> Another fruit or vegetable.
> Bread or cereal: Two servings. Whole-grain bread and cereals preferably, or if not these, enriched bread and enriched or restored cereals.
> Eggs: One egg.
> Meat: One serving. Liver should be eaten at least once a week. Fish, cheese, or dried beans may be eaten occasionally as a substitute for meat.
> A good source of vitamin D: Cod-liver oil or some other source directed by the doctor.
> Additional foods: As needed to meet the demands of the individual woman.
> Water: In liberal amounts.

2. One way of including each of these types of food is shown in the following sample day's menu for a healthy pregnant woman of average weight.

Breakfast

> Fruit: Grapefruit, orange, or other fruit rich in vitamin C.
> Cereal: Whole-grain cereals preferred.
> Bread: Whole-grain or enriched bread with butter or with fortified margarine.
> Milk: A glass of milk, or a cup of cocoa made with milk. Coffee may be taken, if desired, but it should not replace the milk.

Meat: A liberal serving of lean meat.

Vegetables:

A potato, white or sweet.

A cooked vegetable, usually a green leafy vegetable or a deep yellow one.

A raw vegetable; this may be served as a salad.

Bread: Whole-grain or enriched bread with butter or with fortified margarine.

Dessert: Desserts made with milk or fruit should be served often.

Milk: A glass of milk.

Supper or Luncheon

Main dish: A dish made with eggs, or with cheese, or with milk, such as an omelet or rice and cheese.

Vegetable: A cooked vegetable or a salad, depending upon the choice made at other meals.

Dessert: Raw or cooked fruit, with plain cake or cookies.

Milk: A glass of milk.

Cod-liver oil or some other source of vitamin D should be given during pregnancy. The physician will indicate his preference as to the kind and quantity of vitamin D preparation to be given. The daily amount should supply 400 to 800 international units of vitamin D.

The amount of salt commonly used in cooking is sufficient for the expectant mother without the addition of salt at the table. Salty meats and salt fish should be avoided. Fried and highly seasoned foods are apt to cause digestive upsets.

Varied and attractive food, a pleasant environment, a daily program providing outdoor exercise, rest periods and interesting activities, a good social adjustment to the situation—are all factors that improve appetite and utilization of food.

3. The quantity of food needed varies in different individuals. An unusual gain in weight may be due to overeating. If so, a reduction in the total amount of food is usually advisable. In cutting down the total amount of food, however, it is important that there be no reduction in the amounts of the essential foods. The foods that may be safely reduced are some fats, sweets, pastries, and refined cereals and breads.

Frequently there are causes for rapid gain in weight other than overeating. Any sudden marked gain may be a danger signal and should be reported at once to the doctor; it may be due to an accumulation of fluid in the body.

Limiting the amount of food with the idea of having a small infant is not only futile but is even dangerous.

C. Hygiene of pregnancy
(*See* Children's Bureau publication 4, *Prenatal Care.*)

1. Exercise and rest
The amount and kind of housework to be done by the women in the home should not be sufficient to cause fatigue and should be determined for each individual. Reaching, lifting, and pushing heavy things should be avoided. Daily exercise is important for health and the women should have 2 hours outside daily, gardening or walking. No housework or exercise should be continued to the point of fatigue. If varicose veins, swelling of legs, pain in legs and back occur, some limitation of activity may be indicated.

Every pregnant woman should have at least 8 hours sleep at night and a nap or rest period of 1 hour during the day. Fresh air and adequate ventilation in sitting and sleeping rooms promote rest and comfort.

2. Clothing
Dresses should be loose, comfortable, and attractive. Brassieres and abdominal supports should be properly fitted, and usually make the woman more comfortable. Round garters and tight bands should be avoided. Shoes should be comfortably large and have low or medium heels.

3. Care of bowels and kidneys
Adequate diet, fluids, and exercise are aids in overcoming constipation which is a common condition in pregnancy. Eating a variety of fruits, vegetables, and whole-grain products in generous amounts promotes good elimination. The pregnant woman should take a liberal amount of water and other fluids daily. Enemas and laxatives should be given only on the physician's recommendation.

4. Baths and care of skin
The daily bath may be a sponge, shower, or tub bath. Tub baths should be avoided in the last month of pregnancy and should never be taken after labor has begun.

5. Care of breasts
Hygienic care should include softening of crusts on nipples

by use of cold cream. If possible, abnormality of nipples should be corrected during pregnancy.

6. Care of teeth

All needed repairs and extractions should receive attention, preferably during the second trimester of pregnancy. Cleaning the teeth twice daily improves their appearance and the condition of gums and mouth.

7. Mental hygiene

Along with other phases of the program of the home which provide a pleasant and helpful environment for the girls, instruction should be given to prepare them for labor and delivery, so that this experience will not be feared.

8. Complications of pregnancy

Such symptoms as persistent vomiting, repeated headaches, abdominal pains, dizziness, sudden gain in weight, puffiness of face, hands and legs, bleeding or discharges from the vagina, should be immediately reported to the physician and the proper treatment given.

DELIVERY SERVICE

The delivery service in the home or hospital should provide for—

1. Proper care during labor, notification of the physician, arrangement for transferral to hospital or delivery room at the appropriate stage.

There should be constant supervision by a graduate nurse during the stages of labor. Sedation, preparation of the patient for delivery, record of temperature, pulse, and respiration should be carried out according to the physician's directions. The physician should see the patient at intervals during labor: he should be aware at all times of the patient's progress.

Liquid foods with definite nutritive value may be given during the first stage of labor upon the physician's recommendation.

2. The use of sedatives and administration of anesthetic should be under the direction of the physician.

3. The medical and nursing techniques should be in accord with the best obstetric practice. Aseptic operating room technique should be used.

4. Emergency equipment should be available for the administration of oxygen, intravenous fluids, blood transfusions, and for aspiration.

5. Provision should be made for the proper care of the newborn infant.

6. A record of labor and delivery should be kept.

7. When delivery service is given at the maternity home, *a separate unit,* including the delivery room and rooms or wards for mothers and infants should be provided.

8. The delivery room should be used for clean cases only. Patients with infections or communicable conditions should not be delivered in the small maternity home but should be transferred to a hospital where isolation facilities for delivery are available. These would include acute respiratory and contagious diseases —such as pneumonia, influenza, measles—skin infections, open venereal lesions, and intrapartum uterine infections resulting from prolonged labor and rupture of the membranes.

POSTPARTUM CARE

Postpartum care in the home or hospital should provide for—

1. Recovery period following delivery. Every patient, regardless of type of delivery and anesthesia, should have constant nursing attendance until fully conscious. It is well to observe patients in the delivery room for an hour or more. Pulse, blood pressure, height of fundus, amount of bleeding should be noted. If there have occurred any postpartum complications, constant nursing attention should be given. Every postpartum patient should be watched closely for at least 6 hours after delivery because of danger of delayed hemorrhage and shock.

2. Bed rest and bedside nursing care for the first 10 days after delivery. There is special need for rest and sleep following delivery. The patient should be allowed to move freely in bed and perform parts of her toilet. By the third or fourth day the patient may sit up in bed with a back rest for short periods. Most women may sit up in a chair for increasing periods of time from the eighth to fourteenth day, may walk about the room, and have bathroom privileges if bathroom is nearby. After 2 weeks they usually walk about the house and by the end of the third week are allowed to go up and down stairs. For a period of 6 weeks the woman should refrain from full activity.

These are suggestive periods of time for resumption of activity and are to be determined by the physician for the individual case. Mild exercises in bed to tone up the abdominal and general musculature should be carried out as directed by the physician.

3. Individualized nursing care with separate equipment for each patient. Sterile perineal pads, sterile water for perineal cleansing, and a clean bedpan used only for one patient is good procedure. (Bedpans should be sterilized before use by another patient.)

   Thorough and frequent hand-washing by the nurse is essential in giving safe postpartum care. The wearing of masks is considered optional; if worn, masks should be frequently changed, and should not be handled or pulled up and down as is often done.

   No nurse, attendant, or maid with an upper respiratory infection should give care or service to postpartum patients or work in their rooms. This should apply also to physicians.

4. Temperatures to be taken twice daily, or every 4 hours if elevation of temperature occurs. Elevation of temperature should be reported immediately to the physician.

5. A separate room for isolation in case of infection or suspected infection.

6. Immediate reporting of any complications or abnormal symptoms to the physician.

7. A complete medical examination, including a vaginal examination at 6 weeks by the physician.

8. Adequate diet. After full recovery from the anesthetic a general diet may be given as tolerated.

   If the infant is to be breast fed, the total food intake should be increased and more milk added to the mother's diet. The addition of 1 pint of milk (making a total of $1\frac{1}{2}$ quarts of milk), extra servings of vegetables or fruit, a second serving of meat, some increase in bread and cereal, and a little fat will be sufficient. Cod-liver oil or some form of vitamin D should be continued.

9. Breast feeding, if it has been decided advisable for the mother to nurse the child. Instruction as to the care of the breasts, the position of the mother, the technique of feeding the infant should be given by the nurse.

10. Follow-up medical treatment as indicated.

CARE OF INFANTS

(See Children's Bureau publications 292, *Standards and Recommendations for Hospital Care of Newborn Infants,* and 8, *Infant Care.)*

The program for the care of infants in the hospital and in the home should include:

A. **Medical supervision**

   1. Observation of the infant at delivery in regard to respiratory difficulties or abnormalities requiring emergency treatment. Conservation of his body heat is of great importance—a heated crib should be ready to receive him immediately. Prophylactic treatment of the infant's eyes, tying of the cord, and identification should be attended to before the infant is taken from the delivery room.

      Weighing, measuring, bathing should be delayed until later. In transferring the infant from the delivery room, care should be taken to keep him warm.

      The premature infant must have special consideration and care; if the home cannot give the proper care, transfer to a hospital is indicated.

   2. A complete physical examination by the staff pediatrician or physician within the first 24 hours, or sooner if indicated. A repeat examination should be done within the first 10 days.

   3. Close observation by nurse and attendants of all newborn infants, particularly during the first 48 hours.

   4. Examinations and instructions regarding care by the staff pediatrician or physician at the following intervals: every week during the first month, twice during the second month, and once a month during the remainder of the first year. If progress is not satisfactory, change of feeding seems indicated, or abnormality is present, additional examinations, consultation, and appropriate treatment may be needed.

B. **Nursing supervision**

   Care should be supervised by a registered nurse experienced in the care of infants.

C. **Protection from infection**

   1. Individual nursing care. Common bathing and dressing tables should not be used. Strict hand-washing routines should be observed by physician, nurses, and mothers. Hands should be washed with soap and running water before and after handling, diapering, or feeding each infant.

2. Proper care of the skin of newborn infants. This is important in the prevention of infections. It is recommended that no water or oil bath be given for the first 10 days after birth. The vernix may be gently wiped away from the folds of the skin with warm, sterile mineral oil. Linen, diapers, and gowns should be thoroughly clean.

3. Isolation of any infant suspected of having an infection or exposed to infection.

4. Strict limitation of number of persons admitted to nursery. Only those giving care to infants should be allowed in nursery. No person with respiratory or other infection to be admitted.

5. Adequate nursery space so that infants are not crowded together. There should be at least 30 sq. ft. of floor space and 300 cu. ft. of air space per infant. When mothers are cared for in single rooms it is good policy to care for the infant in the same room, moving him out when visitors are admitted.

6. No dry dusting or cleaning of rooms. Wet cloths and mops should be used.

D. Approved feeding procedures
(*See* Children's Bureau publication 8, *Infant Care*, for details.)

1. Breast feeding, unless contra-indicated by medical or social factors. Such factors should be evaluated for each individual mother and baby.

2. Aseptic technique in preparation of milk feeding and other foods. All formulas and changes in feeding to be ordered by the physician.
A separate room or space should be provided for preparation of milk mixtures, other foods, and water. Provision for sterilizing utensils, bottles, and nipples, and adequate refrigeration for storing of milk and food must be made.

3. Babies should be held by nurse, attendant, or mother while being fed; bottles should not be propped up on pillows. Adequate time for sucking should be allowed.

4. Cod-liver oil or some form of vitamin D and orange juice (or grapefruit or tomato juice) should be given in adequate amounts to all infants, and early—by the end of the second week—according to the physician's directions. Other foods should be introduced at the appropriate ages.

E.   Affection and attention

In addition to good medical and physical care, every baby should receive, from an early age, affection and attention according to his age and needs. Impersonal, institutional type of care should never occur.

F.   Clinical records

Medical and nursing records should be kept adequately.

If infants are routinely supervised in child-health conferences, only modified records need be kept in the home.

FACILITIES FOR THE MEDICAL AND NURSING CARE OF MOTHERS

The number and arrangement of rooms and the equipment needed will depend upon the size of the maternity home and the type of services given.

A.   For prenatal care

If prenatal supervision is given by a physician in the home, there should be a room or office used for medical examinations.

Equipment should include examining table, desk, filing cabinet for records, scales, sphygmomanometer for blood pressure readings, pelvimeter for measurements, and equipment for rectal and sterile vaginal examinations, blood counts, Wassermann tests, and urinalyses. Hot and cold running water should be available.

B.   For delivery

There should be a separate unit used only for maternity patients. It should include one or more labor rooms, a delivery room, rooms for postpartum patients, a nursery for newborn infants, and the accessory rooms necessary. The unit should be located in a part of the building away from the regular activities. It should not be used as a passageway or for other purposes when not in use.

1. Labor rooms

These should be single or 2-bed rooms near the delivery room in which the nurse can conveniently observe and care for the patients. Each room should be furnished as a patient's hospital room with bedside table and individual thermometer, bedpan, and toilet articles. The bed should be of the adjustable type with a firm mattress covered with rubber sheeting.

Equipment for carrying out the following procedures should be available on a tray or cart—shaving the perineum, giving an enema, making rectal and sterile vaginal examinations, giving hypodermics, listening to the fetal heart, and taking blood pressure.

If more than one patient is cared for in the same room, screens should be used to insure privacy.

Infected cases should be isolated in a separate room and isolation technique should be observed.

2. Delivery room

Walls, ceiling, and floors should have a smooth and durable finish to permit frequent washing. Windows should be frosted because during delivery they must be closed. There should be diffuse, adequate electric lighting and a portable spotlight. It is desirable to have the delivery room air-conditioned because other methods of ventilation increase danger of air-borne infection.

There should be no flame or open filament in the delivery room because of fire or explosion hazard when volatile anesthetic agents or oxygen are used.

Equipment should include:

a. A delivery table—adjustable, with stirrup attachments.

b. Table for sterile instruments—metal top, rolling type.

c. Facilities for anesthesia—what is needed will depend on the established policies in regard to anesthesia. A small table should be available for the anesthetist.

d. Suction apparatus—with catheter for use for the mother and a suction bulb or ear syringe bulb for use for the infant.

e. Sphygmomanometer and stethoscope

f. Provisions for care of infant:
　　Silver nitrate for eyes
　　Sterile packet for tying cord
　　Heated bassinet, warm blankets
　　Identification method

g. Sterile supplies for delivery—sheets, instruments, basins, gowns.

h. Supply cabinet or shelves for sterile packages, instruments, suture material, syringes, needles, repair sets, intravenous equipment, drugs, and other equipment that should be immediately available in case of emergency. It is preferable that this equipment be near but not in the delivery room.

3. Accessory rooms

    a. Scrub room.—This should adjoin delivery room and be equipped with sink, hot and cold running water, and liquid soap dispenser, all controlled with knee or foot levers, and alcohol basin. A view window between scrub room and delivery room is desirable.

    b. Sterilizing room.—Autoclaves and sterilizers should be provided for sterilization of linens, dressings, instruments, water, and other supplies. They should be checked regularly for adequacy.

    c. Supply room or closet.—For storage of clean linens, sterile packages, instruments, and medications.

    d. Utility room.—This should contain a sink with hot and cold running water, work table, hampers for soiled linen, covered metal waste can, and so on.

    e. Dressing room for doctors.

    f. A nurse's station or desk from which activities are directed, and where records are kept. Dressing room for nurses.

C. For postpartum care

1. Rooms for postpartum care should be located in the maternity unit, so that the nursing service can be centralized and sources of infection guarded against.

2. Running water in each room.

3. Equipment for individual care—bed, bedside table, wash basin, bedpan, thermometer, toilet articles for each patient.

4. Supplies of linen, blankets, sterile perineal pads, masks and gowns conveniently stored.

5. Utility room near patients' rooms, with sink, hopper for emptying and washing bedpans, bedpan sterilizer, hamper for soiled linen.

FACILITIES FOR THE MEDICAL AND NURSING CARE OF INFANTS

What is needed by any home will depend upon the number of newborn infants to be cared for, the policy of using a nursery or caring for them in their mothers' rooms, and the length of time the infants are kept in the home.

A. **Nursery**—for newborn infants up to 6 weeks of age

1. Size

Nursery should be large enough to allow a minimum of 30 sq. ft. of floor space and 300 cu. ft. of air space per infant. Bassinets should be at least 6 inches apart and as much space as possible is desirable.

2. Location, ventilation, lighting, construction

The nursery should be near the maternity rooms, out of the line of traffic. A glass viewing window from the passageway or nurse's station makes possible observation of infants without entering room.

There should be outside windows for lighting and ventilation. Air-conditioning is, of course, desirable. The temperatures should be kept constant at about 80°F, with a relative humidity of 50 percent.

Walls, ceilings, and floors should be washable.

3. Furnishings and equipment

Individual care should be given each infant, which requires for each one a bassinet on stand with bedside table or cabinet where all equipment used for the infant is kept.

An incubator, commercial or home-made, for the care of a premature infant; lavatory with hot and cold water; covered diaper cans; work table, chairs; and linen hampers are required.

Supplies for caring for infants—that is, sterile oil, cotton. blankets, linens, diapers, shirts, gowns, and so forth—are necessities.

Nurses' gowns and masks, mops and materials for cleaning, and laundry facilities—either at a commercial laundry or in a laundry in the home—should be supplied.

B. **Isolation nursery**

For isolation of any infant who is ill or suspected of being ill. If there is no equipped nursery for isolation, a room may be set up for this purpose in the small home with the usual equipment for isolation technique.

C. **Care of infants in mothers' rooms**

The same equipment will be needed for individual care as in the nursery.

676781°—46—6

Only one mother and her infant should be in a room. Individual care and equipment for each infant should be provided as in the nursery for the newborn.

When visitors are present, the newborn infant should be moved out of the room.

D. Care of older infants

There should be a separate nursery for infants over 6 weeks old if they are cared for in the home after that age. It is, however, preferable that they be placed in foster family boarding homes by child-placing agencies.

No infants should be kept in the home past the age of 6 months.

Individual equipment and technique should be continued for infants over 6 weeks of age—with individual tubs for bathing. Running water and a work table will be needed.

If the mother plans to keep her baby, it may be wise for her to care for him in her room from birth until both are ready for discharge.

E. Milk room

There should be a separate room or space for preparing milk mixtures and other foods, used for no other purpose. This room should be divided into two sections—one equipped for washing bottles, nipples, and utensils that have been used and the other for preparing milk mixtures with aseptic technique and for storing them.

Equipment should include: a refrigerator (temperature kept at 40°–45°F), sink, lavatory, sterilizer, bottle warmer, cupboards, and work table.

F. Other space and equipment

The larger homes will need an examining room, nurse's work space, and chart room.

The smaller homes will need to make more use of the space available. Convenient arrangement and good techniques can make possible safe and adequate care without the most expensive equipment.

The Organization of a Home

The focus so far has been on the residents of a home. It is now time to consider the organization that makes possible the services to mothers and babies. This organization is accomplished by civic-minded men and women who, out of interest in this particular community work, join together to sponsor and finance a home and by workers who give the actual service. The theme of this section is the way these two groups, volunteer directors and salaried staff, complement each other to create and foster the services of a maternity home.

THE GROUND WORK[1]

Incorporation

All maternity homes should be incorporated under the laws of the State in which they are established. The law should provide that the secretary of State shall not issue a charter or certificate of incorporation until the authorized department of health or welfare or both shall have

---

[1] *See* Social Agency Boards and How to Make Them Effective, by Clarence King, Harper & Bros., New York 16, N. Y., 1938, 102 pp., and Institutions Serving Children, by Howard W. Hopkirk, Russell Sage Foundation, New York 10, N. Y., 1944, 244 pp.

examined and given approval to the organization applying for incorporation and shall have filed a statement to that effect. The statement should indicate that the department considers such an organization necessary and that the plans for service and for financing are sound.

The advantage of such incorporation is that it enables the responsible State departments to consult with the incorporators before the plan is put into effect. It protects individuals and the community by preventing the incorporation of organizations that are unsound or unnecessary. Furthermore, incorporation protects the individual board members from personal liability for debts incurred by the home. It denotes permanency and responsibility for funds and property. Moreover, Federal and State income taxes make provision for deduction of gifts to charitable corporations. In some States, incorporation is necessary to permit an organization to hold property and to receive bequests.

Constitution and bylaws

The maternity home, like any well-organized body, will have a constitution and bylaws. They should be adapted to the needs of the particular organization but the items usually covered include, in general: The name of the organization; purpose; membership of the corporation; size, selection, duties, and organization of the board of directors; time and place of meetings, and number necessary for a quorum; appointment and duties of committees and staff; and provisions for changes in the constitution. The constitution and bylaws should be studied from time to time for necessary revisions in order to keep them up-to-date. The purpose of the organization should be stated in sufficiently broad terms to permit changes in future years in the services offered. Both constitution and bylaws should be so worded as to facilitate the operation of the organization rather than to retard its progress.

Source of income

The incorporators of a new maternity home should have reasonable assurance of an adequate, continuous flow of funds before beginning to operate. A carefully worked out budget should be prepared yearly by the board of directors and should be of concern to each board member. In addition, accounts of all income and expenditures should be kept and audited regularly by an accredited firm of accountants.

The source of income may be endowment, allotments from the community fund, direct private contributions, payment from public welfare departments on a per capita basis for service rendered, or fees from residents of the home. One State has established a home supported by State funds. More and more frequently maternity homes have been taking part in community-fund campaigns in recent years. This is advantageous to the home and to the total community program because it means that the homes take part in community planning. Furthermore, it relieves the board of the home of the responsibility of raising the budget and it is a sounder method of financing than solicitation by a staff member paid for the purpose.

It is important that unmarried mothers should contribute as much as they can to the cost of their care and the care of their babies. Some mothers can pay the whole fee, although the maximum amount charged by many homes does not nearly cover the cost of the service. Other mothers can pay part of the fee. No mother or baby, however, should be deprived of care for lack of money nor should a girl or her family try to pay more than they can afford.

The unmarried mother should understand clearly in advance the amount she is to pay. She and the case worker can decide this when they talk before the young woman comes to the home. If the application is made by letter, great care should be taken when answering the letter that the details of the financial arrangement do not discourage an unmarried mother without funds from getting the care that she needs.

THE BOARD OF DIRECTORS

The effectiveness of a maternity home as a social organization depends not upon its buildings but upon the caliber of the board of directors and staff and the leadership they give. Their influence is reflected in the atmosphere of the home and in the spirit of the residents.

Functions

The functions of the board of directors depend somewhat on the individual home and the way in which the community is organized to meet its social-service needs. The board is the continuing body ultimately responsible for the home. In general, the directors of a home determine the program, make policies, and establish administrative procedures. They see that the building is kept in good repair and properly equipped. They are responsible for the raising of funds, or for assisting in the community-fund drive, and for the wise expenditure of funds. They choose, advise, and may possibly remove the executive but they delegate to her the details of administration and the execution of plans. They keep closely informed on all major activities in order to be ready to back the executive effectively when necessary. The board should give leadership to the community's program for unmarried mothers. It serves as a nucleus to promote a program and to explain the work to the public in all possible ways.

Michael M. Davis, while director of medical services of the Rosenwald Fund, prepared an excellent list of duties for board members that has been widely used by both public-health and social agencies. The duties are, in part: To know why the organization exists and annually to review why it should; to govern a board or a committee through joint thinking, not by majority vote; to give money, or help get it, or both; to face budgets with courage, endowments with doubt, deficits without dismay, and to recover quickly from a surplus; to deal with members of the professional staff as partners; to keep far enough ahead of the community to be progressive and close enough to be practical; to interpret the work of the agency to the public in words of two syllables; to be proud of a tradition but eager to improve it; and to combine a sense of obligation with a sense of humor.

Basis of selection

Board members should be chosen carefully on the basis of the contribution they can make to the effectiveness of the service. Some of the qualifications that make for valuable board members are intelligence, imagination, enthusiasm, tolerance, open-mindedness, and a willingness to learn and to give time to the duties of membership.

Boards of directors of social organizations profit by having men as well as women members. Although some maternity homes have only women on their boards because of the nature of the service, they would do well to realize that men with a social viewpoint do have a contribution to make in providing service to unmarried mothers and their babies. Men may be chosen for membership who would be particularly helpful on legal, medical, and administrative problems.

Board members should be selected for their ability to give leadership in community activities. Although they should be thoroughly familiar with and convinced of the usefulness of the particular organization they represent, they are even more valuable to it if they are interested in the community welfare program as a whole and if they see clearly the relationship of their own organization to the whole program. This wider interest may be stimulated by having at least a few of the board members of a maternity home serve on the boards of family, children's, or group-work agencies or public-health agencies such as visiting-nurse associations.

Ways of keeping dynamic

A board so organized that new members replace retiring members at regular intervals tends to strengthen the work of the organization by preventing its program from becoming static and by educating a larger number of interested supporters. This addition of new members can be made possible by a provision in the bylaws for the retirement

of a certain number of board members at regular intervals. This may
be done by authorizing appointments for a 3-year term with one-third
of the membership retiring each year. Provision may be made to re-
elect a member after a year of retirement. By such a procedure an
organization is more likely to keep abreast of developments in the fields
of social work and medical care.

The board and staff should be constantly on the alert for individuals
who have the qualifications necessary to promote the services of the
home and who will bring fresh points of view. Although receptivity
to new ideas is not measured by chronological age, every board of
directors will profit by having well-qualified young members.

Number of members

The size of the board is not so important as the qualifications of its
members. Some number of members between 10 and 20 will give a
board that can function most effectively. The exact number will depend
on the organization, type, and size of the home. A representation large
enough to serve as a cross section of the different interests in the community and to carry on the necessary work of subcommittees is a good
basis for determining the size of the board. It should not be so large,
however, as to prevent free discussion and active participation by all
members. Individuals should be chosen for their own worth, but it
is all to the good if they have active connections with professional
groups, service clubs, labor unions, or civic organizations.

Officers and committees

Certain officers and committees are necessary in the administrative
organization of a board. There should be, of course, a president,
selected on the basis of leadership, ability to stimulate and hold the
interest of others, and broad interest in the total planning for social
services in the community.

The treasurer is responsible to the board for the finances of the
home. After the program has been planned for the coming year, a
budget should be developed to provide adequate funds. Full accounts
of money received and disbursed will be audited by a public accountant
at regular intervals. In addition, it will be helpful in informing the
public how the money is spent if the receipts and expenditures can be
analyzed so as to form a clear picture of the cost of the various services.

The secretary is appointed to keep minutes of board meetings and
to take care of the correspondence that has to do directly with the
activities of the board.

To make the board function effectively, certain committees will be
given specific responsibilities. The executive committee can act on
matters that need consideration by a small group before they are pre-

sented to the whole board. This committee can also act in an emergency when it is not possible to arrange for a meeting of the whole membership. It will also carry out certain recommendations of the board.

Other committees will be needed, depending on the way the work of the particular home is organized. Committees encourage participation of individual board members and get certain tasks done that can be handled more expeditiously by a small group. A well-run board, however, does not have to undertake activities that should be handled by the executive of the home or other members of the staff.

Meetings

It is best to hold meetings frequently and at regular intervals. A plan of the points to be discussed or acted upon should be carefully worked out in advance by the president with the help of the superintendent of the home. The superintendent will, of course, attend all board meetings for the full session to present facts about the work of the home and to take part in the discussions. Other members of the staff will be invited to attend when matters are to come up that touch their work. The social worker responsible for case-work service should be present to enter into the discussion when policies and procedures are considered that affect the welfare of mothers and babies. These occasions give the board members a chance to become acquainted with all members of the staff.

Many problems involving the operation of the home will come to the attention of the board. Meetings, however, are more fruitful if they are not devoted entirely to these items. Meetings are opportunities for furthering the board members' understanding of services to unmarried mothers. This understanding may be brought about in a variety of ways. For example, specialists from related professional groups may be invited to speak on certain topics. These talks are particularly helpful if they are followed by discussion. A few suggested topics are: Current trends in case-work philosophy; understanding the adolescent; planning for babies born out of wedlock: resources in the community that can be used by a maternity home, including the specialized services of a psychiatrist or a psychologist; public-health developments; ways in which State departments of health and welfare can assist maternity homes; and new patterns in group-work and leisure-time activities.

Several members of the board might report on current magazine articles or newspaper feature stories that have a bearing on the work of the home. Or a member might report on a visit to a maternity home in another city or on a pertinent lecture or conference he had attended. In other words, if board members are to grow in knowledge and usefulness, they need the nurture given by constant alertness to all that is related to their responsibility and by sharing the results of this alertness with their fellow members.

THE STAFF

Kind and number

The kind and number of staff of a home depend upon the number of mothers and babies cared for, the quality of the care given, and the services obtained through other community resources. A home accommodating as few as from 15 to 30 mothers and babies has the advantage of being able to create a homelike atmosphere. In a small home without hospital facilities, a staff of three is necessary. One person—in most homes known as the superintendent—is in charge. The assistant superintendent is usually responsible when her superior is absent and has direct responsibility for the smooth running of the home in all the aspects of household management.

Because of the nursing service involved in giving prenatal, delivery, and postpartum care to the mothers and care to newborn babies, every home should employ at least one registered graduate nurse. (See *Health and Medical Services* for details on medical and nursing staff.) In some very small homes the position of superintendent and nurse is combined, although this combination does not always make for effective service, centering as it does too much responsibility in one person.

Other workers are needed to do the heavy work of the home and to give the additional service that is necessary at certain times. Their number depends on the number of residents the home can accommodate and whether or not the mothers are delivered of their babies in the home.

Staff members living in close association with unmarried mothers 24 hours a day can either make this experience for the young women a constructive one that justifies the expense of services in time and money, or they can be so unequal to their jobs that they make the residents' stay in the home merely an endurance test. It is important, therefore, for the board to analyze carefully the duties of each staff member and the qualifications necessary for the satisfactory performance of these duties as the first step in filling the positions effectively.

The executive

The superintendent is the person who makes the wheels of administration and program turn. She has to be constantly on the alert for ways to improve the home's policies, procedures, and program. In most homes she has the responsibility for selecting, training, and supervising the other staff members. She is responsible to the board of directors for the satisfactory performance of her staff in their jobs.

Her leadership and enthusiasm carry over to the staff and minimize the tensions that are bound to arise.

The superintendent is in close touch with the board of directors, attending its meetings and submitting reports on various phases of the work in order to keep the directors in touch with the major activities of the home. She will think out ways of sustaining the interest of the board in the whole field of care for unmarried mothers. For example, she may report on meetings and conferences she attends, sharing with the directors the new information and ideas she gains in this way. Or she may stimulate individual board members to join actively in local and State efforts to win more tolerance and more adequate services for unmarried mothers and for children born out of wedlock. She and the case worker together, because of their close relationship with the mothers in the home, are responsible for making clear to the board the needs of the residents for special services.

The superintendent is responsible also for the supervision of all aspects of the housekeeping, including the planning of nutritious meals under instructions of the physician for amounts and kinds of food required by pregnant women. Many of the young women in the home will not be in the best physical condition when they enter and will need especially nutritious food to prepare them to go through pregnancy and delivery and to have healthy babies. (See *Health and Medical Services.*)

The training and previous experience of the superintendent are important. She need not be a nurse, teacher, or social worker; she must know when to call on specialists and how to utilize their services. It would be helpful if all superintendents could have some professional training in social work or at least some experience in a case-work agency of high standards. If the superintendent is a nurse, it would be helpful if she had professional training and experience as a public-health nurse. Any shortage of case workers and nurses, however, will make these requirements impracticable. More important than ever, therefore, is the ability of the superintendent, whatever her qualifications, to distinguish between the work she is equipped to do and the assistance she must obtain from professionally educated specialists.

In this division of labor, less confusion will probably arise in regard to the physical care of the mothers than in the social planning for their welfare and the welfare of the babies. This point has been discussed earlier in *The Value of Case-Work Service,* but it can be reemphasized here that the superintendent, engrossed in the responsibility of running the home, is likely to have neither time nor energy, even if she had qualifications, to give case-work service.

A superintendent is most useful to the home if she appreciates various professional skills and knows when to accept professional opinion without question. Although no superintendent would question a physician's judgment about the necessity for surgery, some superintendents fail to recognize the value of other professional judgment on matters that will chart the course for the whole future of mother and child. They also fail to realize the interdependence of medical and social skills in giving a mother the best possible basis for her decisions. It is a superintendent's responsibility to see that all phases of the young woman's problems are considered professionally.

The superintendent's personal qualifications are of great consequence. Broad cultural interests will help a superintendent to bring new interests to the residents of the home and to be effective in her relationships with staff, members of the board, and others in the community.

One of the most significant—and least tangible—phases of the superintendent's work is her relationship with the young women in the home. Many of them are very young and many have had an unhappy relationship with their own mothers. Some of this latter group will look to the superintendent for the kind of refuge and strength they would expect from their mothers. She will become to them a person to admire and to pattern themselves after. Without realizing it, perhaps, their trust in her grows out of her ability to accept them at their current stage of development and out of her complete freedom from desire to punish them by word or deed for a point of view or behavior different from her own standard of conduct.

The ideal executive of a home is the kind of person who can quickly establish a friendly relationship with others. She is mature emotionally but is not necessarily old in years. She is sensitive to the feelings of others and realizes the meaning of an adolescent's deviation from normal behavior. Her understanding of the difficulties an unmarried mother has faced and will face makes her tolerant of aggressive behavior in the home. She knows how to help the residents individually and how at the same time to promote the welfare of the group. She knows when holding to regulations is essential to the smooth running of the home, and when modifying them in the interest of an individual mother in a specific situation is wise. Her fundamental approach is one of helpfulness.

Personnel practices

The personal qualifications of the other staff members should be similar to those of the superintendent in many ways, because they also have close association with the residents of the home. The vocational skills of the others will vary, however, because of the different tasks that they are employed to do. (For the responsibilities of the medical and nursing staff see the section, *Health and Medical Services.*)

If a home is to have a well-qualified staff, the conditions of employment must be such as to make the work a satisfying experience. Such procedures as arrangements for vacations, sick leave, and accident insurance coverage that are in keeping with the policies of other social agencies in the community should be explained at the time a staff member is employed. The board of directors should follow consistently the practice of handling all matters directly with the superintendent, instead of taking them up directly with other staff members. Likewise, the superintendent should be responsible to the entire board rather than to any one member or one committee. Unless basic considerations like these are adhered to, the staff can easily be at the beck and call of a number of different directors—perhaps making conflicting requests.

Staff members who live at the home should have comfortable quarters and as much privacy as possible. Working hours should be reasonable. It would be well if arrangements could be made for staff members to spend at least one regular day a week and one week-end a month away from the home. If this particular arrangement is not convenient, some reasonable amount of free time should be allotted regularly so that staff members may return to the home refreshed. Additional persons should be planned for to take the places of the workers who are away.

THE BUILDINGS AND GROUNDS

The plant and equipment of a maternity home are of consequence to its program. They influence the ease with which work can be done and, in general, create the atmosphere of the home. The type of buildings and equipment, however, is not so important as the way in which the two are used. Some homes are giving excellent service in plants that are old and unsuited to their present use. Others have modern, well-equipped buildings but outmoded programs for the residents that are out of keeping with the excellence of their physical plants. The spirit of the home is its value.

Kinds of buildings

Many homes are at present housed in buildings that are not designed for this purpose; they were formerly private residences. Some of these houses may be well adapted to their current use, but others may lack facilities to give proper care to pregnant women and to babies. This is particularly true if the home attempts to provide delivery service rather than to send the mothers to a hospital. In addition, the living quarters may be inadequate and inconvenient. There may be too few bathrooms, stairs may be too steep, and living and sleeping quarters may be overcrowded. The advantage of using a former residence is that the number of young women accepted is usually small and the place can have the atmosphere of a family home rather than of an institution.

All laws and regulations having to do with fire hazards and health should be observed with particular care in these remodeled buildings. These protections should, of course, be assured in all homes but are easier to accomplish in a building designed as a maternity home.

Another type of building used for the care of unmarried mothers is obviously institutional. Such a "home" may be a unit in itself, set apart in a suburban section or in the midst of a crowded city district, or it may be one unit of an institution that also has a maternity hospital and a home for infants. Although this latter arrangement may be very satisfactory because the building can be made homelike, it is more apt to have grave disadvantages that require wise planning to overcome. These institutions are usually located on downtown streets that were formerly residential or in neighborhoods that have deteriorated since the institution was founded and are no longer suitable for the program. Furthermore, housing the unmarried mothers in part of the institution offers a temptation to have them do the household work of the other units. This plan may be advantageous to the institution but defeats the true social purpose of a maternity home. An even less desirable place for group care of unmarried mothers is one wing or a separate floor of a hospital.

Maternity homes are located in all kinds of neighborhoods, it has just been pointed out, some obviously unsuited as places of residence for young unmarried mothers. The home should be in a location in which the mothers can feel comfortable on the streets and can be free to go and come unaccompanied by a member of the staff.

The grounds of the home, although they need not be large, should be large enough to permit the entire group of mothers to spend much of their leisure time out of doors and to give the babies their quota of fresh air. It is an advantage if the grounds are large enough for recreational equipment. Trees, shrubs, and flowers will make the garden space attractive. This attractiveness can be accomplished without too great an expenditure of money if space and soil permit and especially if some member of the board has the imagination and enthusiasm to promote the project.

Interior of a home

The rooms of the building should be decorated and furnished in good taste in a way to be as inviting and homelike as possible. Anyone who has visited a good number of homes will have flashes of memory of some cheerful spot in some particular home that have nothing to do with a modern building or expensive furnishings but everything to do with homemaking ability. Memory may recall a sunshine-flooded dining room furnished with small tables for four. The bright windows are curtained in excellent taste and the walls and furniture are painted a soft, pleasant color. A room young women would like—and do. Or memory may show again the wonders done in a huge dormitory that used to house the mothers *en masse.* The big room has high ceilings and good ventilation and its wide open spaces have been transformed into small bedrooms by the use of temporary walls. These airy, cheerful bedrooms have become "home" to many a young woman who never before knew the privacy of a room of her own or had even a place to put her possessions.

Although these pictures are of physical backgrounds, they reflect the thoughtfulness of those who direct a home towards its residents in trying to make a livable, pleasing atmosphere in spite of adverse housing conditions. Even in old buildings ingenuity, a knowledge of color values for choosing curtain materials and paint for woodwork, and a sense of simplicity in decoration that makes the total effect of color and design in the home a unity can make the difference between a drab, repelling interior and a welcoming one.

The rooms of a home

Certain rooms are required to carry on the activities of a home. Space and equipment for the health and medical program are listed in detail in another section, *Health and Medical Services.* This discussion is of the other quarters.

The superintendent will need an office in which privacy is assured for interviews with residents and staff members. She will need a desk, of course, and lockable files for records and other confidential papers. If the home employs its own case worker, she, too, should have an office in which the mothers would feel free to talk to her about confidential matters.

Some homes will have their own chapels, around which the religious activities of the residents center. Other homes will use the living room for religious services and other gatherings. For this reason, the living room should be large enough to accommodate easily the whole number of residents. It might well have comfortable davenports and chairs and the other furnishings that a family home has when the homemaker gives thought and time to her family's convenience and pleasure. This room should have a piano, radio, phonograph, and plenty of records of music that young women would like. Readable books and magazines suited to different grades of intelligence and types of interest should be readily accessible.

One smaller room, and preferably more than one, should be set aside for young women to read and write letters, listen to music away from the group or entertain their friends. The larger homes, especially those built for their present purpose, should have a recreation room with suitable equipment. Smaller homes may have to combine the living and recreation rooms.

A pleasant dining room is a necessity. Tables for four are desirable, shared by staff members and residents. Mealtime should be cheerful—not a time to settle the problems of the day.

Many who are interested in maternity-home care believe that each resident should have her own bedroom. This not only insures privacy and the rest that is required in pregnancy, but gives a young woman a sense of pride in caring for her room that she can carry over into her own home later. Many of the unmarried mothers have lived in such crowded homes that they have never known what it means to have one spot they can call theirs. A resident should feel free to spend time in her own room and to have her own things there. Each resident will need, as a minimum in the way of furniture, her own bed, chest of drawers, mirror, and chair. If she does not bring toilet articles with her, inexpensive but attractive ones should be given to her to keep.

One argument advanced against single rooms is that unmarried mothers may become morose and lonely in rooms of their own. The answer is that if a mother is in a depressed state, she needs assistance from a case worker or a psychiatrist rather than the company of a room mate. The home that has an adequate program of activities and a happy, friendly atmosphere will have few young women who fear to be alone. (See *New Interests Through Group Activities*.) If single rooms are impossible in a home, not more than two or three residents should have to share a room. Some of the older, institutional type of homes, built when dormitories were in vogue, may be able to divide the space into single rooms by partitions. Even screens or curtains are preferable to one large open space, but care is required to insure satisfactory ventilation.

Fully adequate bath and toilet facilities should be located conveniently near the bedrooms. Both tubs and showers are desirable. one or the other to be used in accordance with the physician's recommendation. Even the detail of having enough towel racks is of consequence.

Suitable living quarters will, it has been said, be provided for the staff to insure as much privacy and quiet as possible. In some homes a common living room for the staff seems best, but in others, the staff may prefer to have day beds so that they may use their rooms as sitting rooms. A chance to relax and rest in comfort for even short periods of time means a great deal to workers who live where they work.

Efficient food service calls for not only a well-arranged kitchen but a separate room for storing staple and canned goods, adequate refrigeration facilities, and provision for prompt disposal of garbage and other waste. Good lighting and proper ventilation make it possible to work with a minimum of fatigue. Plumbing and facilities for storing and handling food should conform to local sanitary regulations, copies of which are available from the department of health.

If residents are to participate in food preparation and serving, extra care should be given to removal of accident hazards. Even in homes that are not equipped with modern facilities and that have little money to spend on improvements, good planning will eliminate or greatly reduce the number of accidents caused by swinging doors, slippery floors, and unprotected equipment.

Other rooms may be necessary in addition to those mentioned, depending on the program of the home. Some homes for instance, will equip schoolrooms if young girls are accepted for care and if the home finds it possible to get a satisfactory teacher.

* * *

Have maternity homes kept pace during the last 6 decades with the advances in social and medical sciences to which they are allied, especially in the understanding of human behavior as it has developed in these fields? That question is not meant to be answered, of course, because in none of the factors can the advance be measured accurately enough to warrant comparison. But the thought behind the question may be seen constantly between the lines of this bulletin. The pages suggest some specific goals for strengthening the services given to unmarried mothers in maternity homes. The goals are quite obtainable with good planning. They are, in brief, to utilize for the residents sound advances in social service, obstetric and pediatric medicine, and the results of psychiatric research through the practical applications available.

Maternity homes, beginning as places of refuge that shut themselves away from the life of the cities surrounding their walls, are now becoming an articulate force in influencing social justice. What group knows better than their directors and staffs how unfair the world can be to unmarried mothers and to boys and girls who start out in life with the heavy, society-placed burden of illegitimate birth?

For sale by the Superintendent of Documents, U. S. Government Printing Office
Washington 25, D. C. · Price 20 cents

Milton Keynes UK
Ingram Content Group UK Ltd.
UKHW041418031123
431899UK00004B/573

9 789354 027871